Adventures in
IMPROV QUILTS

Master Color,

CINDY GRISDELA

C&T PUBLISHING

Text copyright © 2021 by Cindy Grisdela

Photography and artwork copyright © 2021 by C&T Publishing, Inc.

Publisher: Amy Barrett-Daffin

Creative Director: Gailen Runge

Acquisitions Editor: Roxane Cerda

Managing Editor: Liz Aneloski

Editor: Kathryn Patterson

Technical Editor: Julie Waldman

Cover/Book Designer: April Mostek

Production Coordinator: Tim Manibusan

Production Editor: Alice Mace Nakanishi

Illustrator: Linda Johnson

Photo Assistants: Lauren Herberg and Gabriel Martinez

Photography by Estefany Gonzalez of C&T Publishing, Inc., unless otherwise noted

Published by C&T Publishing, Inc.,
P.O. Box 1456, Lafayette, CA 94549

Library of Congress Cataloging-in-Publication Data

Names: Grisdela, Cindy, 1958- author.

Title: Adventures in improv quilts : master color, design & construction / Cindy Grisdela.

Description: Lafayette, CA : C&T Publishing, [2021]

Identifiers: LCCN 2021009387 | ISBN 9781644030691 (trade paperback) | ISBN 9781644030707 (ebook)

Subjects: LCSH: Quilting--Design. | Patchwork--Design. | Improvisation in art.

Classification: LCC TT835 .G76538 2021 | DDC 746.46--dc23

LC record available at https://lccn.loc.gov/2021009387

Printed in the USA

10 9 8 7 6 5 4 3 2

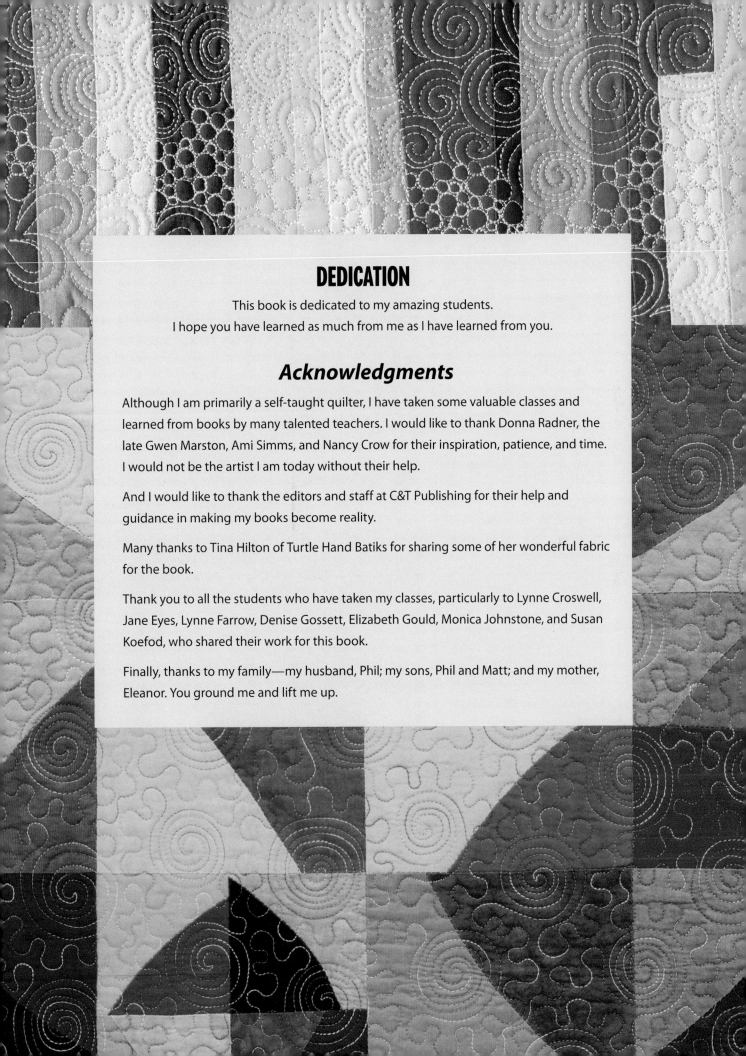

DEDICATION

This book is dedicated to my amazing students.
I hope you have learned as much from me as I have learned from you.

Acknowledgments

Although I am primarily a self-taught quilter, I have taken some valuable classes and learned from books by many talented teachers. I would like to thank Donna Radner, the late Gwen Marston, Ami Simms, and Nancy Crow for their inspiration, patience, and time. I would not be the artist I am today without their help.

And I would like to thank the editors and staff at C&T Publishing for their help and guidance in making my books become reality.

Many thanks to Tina Hilton of Turtle Hand Batiks for sharing some of her wonderful fabric for the book.

Thank you to all the students who have taken my classes, particularly to Lynne Croswell, Jane Eyes, Lynne Farrow, Denise Gossett, Elizabeth Gould, Monica Johnstone, and Susan Koefod, who shared their work for this book.

Finally, thanks to my family—my husband, Phil; my sons, Phil and Matt; and my mother, Eleanor. You ground me and lift me up.

CONTENTS

INTRODUCTION

Blue Puzzle by Cindy Grisdela, 21˝ × 24˝, 2020

As an artist, I believe it's important to continue to explore new ideas and to be open to growth and change. If you're reading this book, I hope you feel the same way.

I was fortunate as a child that my parents recognized my interest in art and encouraged it. I always had crayons and paper, and as I grew older, classes in drawing, painting, and ceramics. My mother taught me to sew when I was about ten, and I had a great aunt who took me under her wing around the same time and taught me embroidery, cross-stitch, needlepoint, and knitting. I used my electives in high school to take art and art history classes, and when it was time to go to college, I chose to major in art history. But there weren't any quilters in my family, and I didn't know anything about quilting until I happened to see an article in a women's magazine as a college student.

After graduating from college with a BA in fine arts, I went to work for several small financial firms to pay the bills. I have always been interested in business as well as art, so I went back to school to get an MBA in finance. I ended up working for Dow Jones News Service as a financial reporter for a number of years, then took time off to raise my sons. My creative pursuits were limited to evenings and weekends.

I couldn't get that quilting article out of my mind, and I kept it for a couple of years until I had time to try my hand at quilt making. My first efforts were less than successful, but creating with fabric and thread, color and texture was inspiring to me in a way that none of my previous artistic explorations had been. My husband comes from a family of eight children and I'm the oldest of four, so there were lots of baby quilts to make to refine my skills at piecing and hand quilting. With each one, I tried some new pattern or technique. I'm sure most of those quilts are in shreds by now and that's probably for the best!

I began my Improv journey more than ten years ago after nearly two decades as a traditional quilter, but the seeds of that journey were present long before I made the leap. I always enjoyed making scrappy quilts and I was particularly intrigued with Amish quilts for their color and graphic design punch.

I gave away many of the early quilts I made, but *Moody Blues* is an example of my scrappy approach to traditional quilts. The pattern is known as Corn and Beans and it's most often made in yellows and greens. I chose to make mine in blues, my favorite color at the time, using a variety of small-scale prints. My Amish-style *Double Nine-Patch* (page 17) is another early example.

Moody Blues by Cindy Grisdela, 56″ × 56″, 2001
An early traditional quilt

Arranging Improv blocks on a design wall
Photo by Gregory R. Staley

I am indebted to a number of teachers for their inspiration, either in person or in their books. Donna Radner, the late Gwen Marston, Ami Simms, and Nancy Crow all helped me to chart my own journey. Donna helped me understand how to use color in a dynamic way back in the beginning, Gwen liberated me from rules through her books, Ami helped me to embrace free-motion quilting, and Nancy pushed me to approach quilt design as artistic design. My profound thanks to all of them and to others who inspired me along the way.

Maybe you're just beginning your Improv journey, or you've experimented with some of the techniques and you're interested in new design ideas. With this book, I hope to inspire you to move forward on your creative journey with three different ways to create improvisationally. I start with an expanded look at multiple-cut curves, dig into ways to combine block units to create compelling designs, and discuss free cutting your lines and shapes and designing the entire quilt on the wall before sewing.

This book builds on the skills and techniques found in my first book, *Artful Improv* (page 95), but you don't have to use them in sequence. Try something new, embrace your mistakes and learn from them, explore your quilting DNA and use it to strengthen your creative muscles, and be fearless with color.

Let's get started!

how to use
THIS BOOK

Red Rover by Cindy Grisdela, 29″ × 37″, 2020

This is a resource book for Improv design. I hope it will inspire you to create your own original quilts by looking at color and design in a new way, examining your quilting history to help you focus on your strengths, and trying some new techniques or putting familiar elements together differently.

We all create original work in our own style, because we all have different likes and dislikes, quilting history, and experience. Your style is like your fingerprint, unique to you. No one else can create the same design in the same way as you do.

Lime Medley by Cindy Grisdela, 26″ × 37″, 2016
Leftover blocks get new life.
Photo by Gregory R. Staley

I am known for my approach to color. But I wasn't always fearless about color—in fact, in the beginning I was downright timid. Blues were my comfort zone, and I made lots of blue quilts for many years. There's nothing wrong with exploring your comfort zone for a while, but I hope some of the concepts in this book will encourage you to step outside that zone, even if it's just to add a different spark to a familiar color palette.

There are no patterns as such here, since that's not what Improv design is, but I have provided four guided exercises in cutting curves and putting multiple units together into new compositions to jump-start your imagination.

I encourage you to try new color combinations and put elements together differently than you may have in the past, make your own rules and guidelines, and embrace your uniqueness. Be open to the possibilities and put aside fear—fear of doing it wrong, fear of not being perfect or even good enough, fear of rejection.

There are no mistakes in Improv, just opportunities to create a different design. Thomas Edison is reported to have said about his efforts to invent the light bulb, "I have not failed. I've just found 10,000 ways that won't work."

You may make some units or even some quilt tops that aren't your favorites, but you can add to them, or cut them up, or put them in your leftover basket to look at another day. I don't throw away any blocks or units, even if I hate them. You never know when a fresh look will make the difference and that discarded block can become the basis for a new composition.

Lime Medley was created almost entirely from leftover blocks from previous projects, and a certain sherbet green fabric that didn't go well with anything else ever. I challenged myself to make something from what I had, and it worked.

what is IMPROV?

Happy Days by Cindy Grisdela, 27˝ × 27˝, 2018

mprov is short for improvisation, and it refers to a free-form design strategy to create artistic quilts with no patterns and no templates. Improv is a great way to showcase your own voice as an artist.

Improv quilts are often abstract and contemporary, but not always. Many of the wonderful scrap quilts our grandmothers made could be considered Improv, because they improvised with the materials they had available to them—worn out clothes, feed sacks, and odds and ends from the scrap basket—to make coverings to keep their families warm. Certainly, the quilts of Gee's Bend could be considered Improv. The unique works made by these African-American quilters from a remote community in Alabama explode with energy.

Improv quilts can be controlled, or wild, or anywhere in between. Some Improv quilts are based on block designs, similar to traditional block-based quilts, and others are completely free-form.

Happy Days is a block-based Improv quilt that uses a fairly controlled organizing principle. I created the blocks individually and used stripes both to cope with sections where the blocks didn't fit exactly, and to add interesting lines and shapes to the design.

Blue Confetti by Cindy Grisdela, 46″ × 47″, 2019
Free-cut curves without a ruler or templates

In contrast, I designed *Blue Confetti* entirely on the design wall, improvising the lines and shapes as I went with chunks of fabric before I sewed anything together.

No Rules in Improv

There are no rules in Improv, except those you decide for yourself. Typically, I make only two decisions before starting a new Improv quilt—what color palette I'm going to use and the approximate size I want the finished quilt to be.

The idea of creating without patterns or templates can be a little daunting at first, but there's a lot of freedom in this approach. For one thing, there's no way to make a mistake! That's one of the first things I tell students in my Improv classes, and you can see the smiles and the sighs of relief right away.

Not all of your blocks will be interesting enough to fit into the finished quilt, but each block and each quilt is an opportunity to learn something new—about the process and about yourself as an artist. It's one of the things I like best about creating improvisationally; there's always something new to explore, even if you've been creating this way for a while. Maybe it's a new color combination, a new texture, or a different way of working. And the castoffs can always go into your leftover basket, where one or more of them might be just the right thing for a new project later.

I had a student in class a few years ago who wasn't happy with an Improv Log Cabin block she made. It turned out she liked one side of the block but didn't care for the other side. I told her to cut off the side she didn't like and keep the rest. "You can do that?!" she asked excitedly. Yes, you absolutely can.

Ask "What If?"

Asking "What if?" is a crucial part of the process. Because there's no pattern to follow, you get to decide what goes where. What if I group all the blocks with white in them in the center of the design, like *Happy Days* (pages 11 and 39)? What if I add lime green for a spark of contrast, like *Hint of Lime*? What if I turn the piece upside down or sideways? What if I add patterned fabric to the mix of solids, or vice versa?

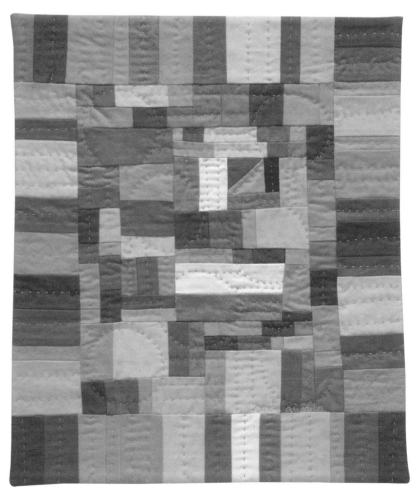

Hint of Lime by Cindy Grisdela, 17˝ × 19˝, 2010
One small strip of lime adds the spark.

Leave your work up on a design wall while you decide what comes next.
Photo by Gregory R. Staley

Use a Design Wall

Improv is not a quick process. It's important to use some kind of design wall, so you can give your work time to rest while you do something else and it won't be disturbed by the kids or the cat. It can be as simple as a piece of batting tacked up to the wall, or it can be a permanent part of your studio setup.

I take lots of photos of work in process. Sometimes looking at a photo helps me to see problem areas more clearly than looking at the design in front of me. Also, it gives me a reference if I change an element and then decide I want to put things back the way they were.

My design wall is made of 24˝ squares of foam insulation board that you can find at a home improvement store. I covered the squares with batting and attached them to the wall, so they are always available to me. I tend to work on several different projects at once and having a large design wall is essential. That way when I get stuck on one design, I leave it up on the wall to marinate while I work on something else. Sometimes the solution to the first design issue comes from working on the second one.

where to START?

Radiance by Cindy Grisdela, 16″ × 20″, 2018

Choose Color and Size

As I mentioned in the last chapter, when I begin an Improv project, I make two decisions right away—what colors and what size. The rest will come as a result of the decisions I make as the process unfolds.

I'll talk more about color choice in Choosing a Color Palette (page 23), but for now, I just decide if I want to use warm colors like red, orange, and yellow; cool colors like green, blue, and purple; or maybe a neutral palette with cream, beige, and tan. As I go along, I almost always change or add colors and values, but it helps to have a starting point. Each choice depends on the mood or sensibility you would like to convey. Quilts with warmer colors are usually more energetic, while cooler colors are often more calming.

For size, I mark out the anticipated size with blue painter's tape on my design wall. Improv quilts often involve a number of seams that shrink the final com-position, and it helps to know right on the design wall where the edges should be. You can also pin narrow strips of fabric to the wall to show the anticipated size. Of course, these aren't hard and fast rules, just a suggestion to follow so the quilt doesn't end up being smaller than you intended. This is especially important if you're creating something to enter in an exhibit with size requirements. You can improvise as the process unfolds if you decide the size you origi-nally wanted needs to be smaller or larger.

At this point, you may or may not have an idea of what you want the quilt to look like. Maybe you want to work with Improv Log Cabin blocks, or big curves, or stripes. Generally, I just dive right in, cutting my shapes directly out of the fabrics and either putting them up on the design wall, or sewing them together in units that will be arranged later. But if you prefer to start with a rough sketch or drawing to keep your idea in front of you, that's fine too.

Your Quilting DNA

As I've traveled the country teaching and lecturing the last few years, it's become clear to me that each of us has our own likes and dislikes, preferences, and bugaboos. I call this our quilting DNA. I like small shapes, scrappy asymmetrical designs, bright colors, and intricate free-motion quilting. This has been true of my quilts from the beginning of my quilting journey many years ago, except for the free-motion quilting part—I was a hand quilter in the beginning.

Recently a studio redesign found me with a pile of UFOs from years ago. I was stunned to see that the quilts I was making nearly 30 years ago had much in common with the quilts I'm making now.

I began this Amish-inspired *Double Nine-Patch* quilt about 25 years ago, started to hand quilt it, got distracted, and put it away. When I rediscovered it recently, I was surprised to see that the small Nine-Patch blocks were created very randomly—some had just two colors, as is usual with Nine-Patch blocks, but many of them took a scrappier approach. I decided to leave the hand quilting in and finish it by machine so I could use it on the sofa.

A look at the back is even more startling. I wasn't using many solid fabrics back then, so I wanted to use up what I had on the back. The pieced back of this quilt echoes my current work surprisingly well.

You may like larger blocks and shapes, fewer fabrics in each unit or quilt, and more symmetrical designs. That's okay. It's important to understand what your quilting DNA is so you don't try to force yourself into a style that doesn't fit. There's a difference between trying something new to see if you enjoy it and think-ing that you "should" do things a certain way just because a teacher or friend says that's the way it has to be done.

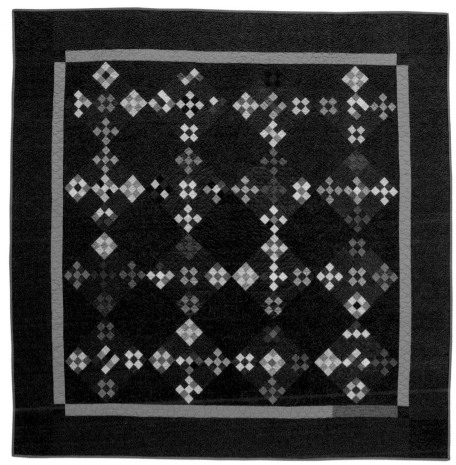

Double Nine-Patch by Cindy Grisdela, 62″ × 62″, 2020

Early Amish-inspired quilt using scraps and solid fabrics

There's room in Improv for many different ways of working—smaller or larger, symmetrical or not, free-form or more controlled. And, of course, solids or prints. That's one of the benefits of working this way. There is no "one size fits all." You get to decide how the pieces fit together according to your own style.

One of the things I like most about teaching Improv is that each student will come out of my class with a quilt top that is different from his or her neighbor's and different from my work as well, even though each student is taught the same techniques.

The back of *Double Nine-Patch* has an Improv feel.

Solids Versus Prints

So, what about the question of solids versus prints?

I use solid fabrics in my work because I like the graphic nature of designs created with solid fabrics. The lines and shapes are distinct, and somehow more painterly, than designs created with prints. Prints tend to merge and blur the lines of the composition, which is fine if that's the effect you are striving for. In addition, the pattern of a print can be a distraction from the design you're trying to create.

Balloon Fiesta by Cindy Grisdela, 19˝ × 27˝, 2018

Solid fabrics create graphic appeal in a warm color scheme.

Snow in Winter by Cindy Grisdela, 15˝ × 25˝, 2017

Print fabrics give a different look to a similar design.

Balloon Fiesta and *Snow in Winter* are two quilts made with the same idea in mind, but the effect is very different. The lines and shapes in *Balloon Fiesta*, made completely with solid fabrics, are more defined, while those in *Snow in Winter* are less distinct, particularly on the center right. Neither is right or wrong. What's important is that you as the artist convey the impression you want to make.

There is a middle ground. Sometimes printed fabrics can be the spark that adds a nice contrast to the design. These batiks from Turtle Hand Batik add interesting lines to a mostly solid design.

Printed batik fabrics add interest to mostly solid blocks.

See the contrast of the two quilts below: *Neon Fizz*, which is composed of only solids, and *Autumn Curves*, which combines solids with prints. The solid fabrics in *Autumn Curves* are also from several different manufacturers—commercial solids from Kona Cotton (by Robert Kaufman Fabrics), hand-dyed solids from Cherrywood Fabrics, and shot cottons (where the warp and weft are different colors) from Oakshott Fabrics. There are no rules about how and when you can combine fabrics in Improv design.

Neon Fizz by Cindy Grisdela, 32˝ × 32˝, 2019

A controlled color palette in solid fabrics lets lines and shapes shine.

Autumn Curves by Cindy Grisdela, 32˝ × 32˝, 2019

Combining prints with solids

Another consideration about using printed fabrics involves the quilting. The stitching lines show up much better on solid fabrics than they do on printed ones. That was one of the reasons I began using more solids in my work. As my free-motion stitching got better, I wanted the work I put in to add texture to my designs to show up in the finished pieces. You can see the effect in *Finger Painting*. The focus is the pieced design and the stitching is secondary.

Finger Painting by Cindy Grisdela, 12˝ × 12˝, 2019

Focus on printed fabrics

Organizing Fabrics

Organizing fabric is a very personal choice. Your fabric collection is your paint—the raw material you use to create your art—so it's important to use a system that makes sense to you so you can find what you need when you need it.

I keep my fabric in wire runner baskets that live beneath my cutting surface and my ironing station, so the spaces do double duty. The fabrics are sorted roughly by color and by type, so my red batiks are separate from my red solids, for example. As my stash of prints shrinks and my collection of solids grows, I've further subdivided the solids by hand-dyed and commercial fabrics, so my Cherrywood Fabrics hand-dyed solids are separate from the solids from Kona Cotton (by Robert Kaufman Fabrics) or Art Gallery Fabrics. Whatever organization choice you make will depend on your personal fabric collection and preferences.

Fabric stored in wire baskets by color and type
Photo by Gregory R. Staley

Ironing station and inspiration board with fabric storage underneath
Photo by Gregory R. Staley

Using Leftovers

Improv design can result in leftover blocks and scraps, since you often make more units than you need and sometimes cut shapes that don't work in the design. Don't throw them away! I keep these blocks and scraps in baskets on my cutting table. The scraps are sorted generally by color and the leftovers go in their own basket.

Baskets of scraps live on my cutting table.

Leftover blocks may end up in another quilt later.

The scraps are great idea generators for Improv blocks. Often, I just dump out a basket of scraps and start sewing. *Radiance* was the result of one of these sessions, where I sewed warm and cool scraps into Improv blocks to create something new and interesting.

Leftover blocks, stripes, curves, and trimmings from other projects can sometimes be the beginnings of a new composition. *Metamorphosis* was made almost entirely from leftovers from other designs.

Radiance by Cindy Grisdela, 16″ × 20″, 2018

Scraps as inspiration

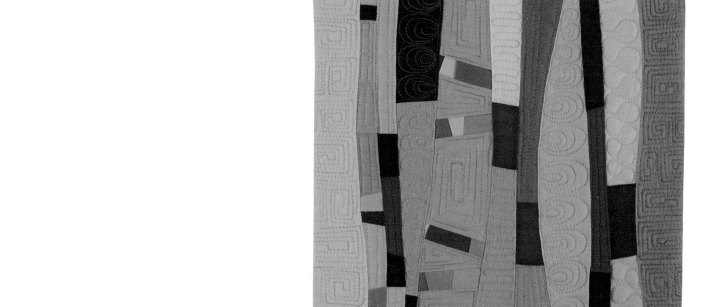

Metamorphosis by Cindy Grisdela, 12″ × 12″, 2017

Various stitching motifs add interest to a scrappy design.

Photo by Gregory R. Staley

choosing a
COLOR PALETTE

Playing with Colors by Cindy Grisdela, 45˝ × 54˝, 2008

Purple flowers against green foliage show nature's color combinations at work, complemented by the orange and black butterflies.

Photo by Dorry Emmer

olor is one of the enduring joys of life. I can remember as a child lying on my stomach on the floor with a box of crayons, carefully choosing possible color combinations before starting in on a project in a coloring book, or later a sketchbook.

Rows of vegetables or fruits at a farmer's market can be feasts for the eye as well as the table. And a garden can be a limitless source of inspiration, from the bright colors of flowers to the subtle shades in leaves and branches.

What is the first thing you see when you look at a quilt or other piece of art? Often, it's the color. That's how important color can be in the appeal of your design. But how do you use color effectively?

Going back to the idea of quilting DNA, we all have our own personal histories with color. Maybe you revel in color and its possibilities. Or maybe choosing color is a bit scary for you and you worry about doing it wrong. Maybe you've made a lot of blue quilts, like I did in the beginning, or you never, ever use orange.

Choosing color is intuitive for some people and a chore for others. I wasn't confident about my color sense in the beginning and I made quite a few bland quilts as a result before I figured it out.

The good news is you can teach yourself to be better at choosing colors for your quilts.

The Color Wheel

Let's start with the basics.

There are three primary colors—red, blue, and yellow. Combining these colors gives you secondary colors—orange, green, and purple. Further combinations produce the tertiary colors of yellow-orange, blue-green, and red-violet.

You can see the myriad combinations in a color wheel.

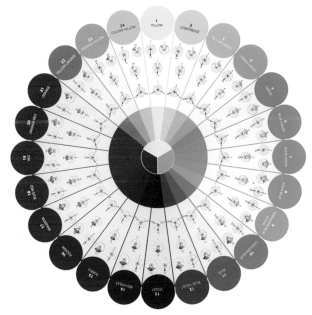

A color wheel, such as Joen Wolfrom's Essential Color Wheel Companion (by C&T Publishing), can be a useful design tool.

Although it can seem a little daunting, a color wheel is often an excellent resource when you'd like to try a new-to-you color combination, or if you want to look at options to spice up a design you're working on.

It may help to define a few terms. You can think of color in terms of its hue, saturation, temperature, and value.

A color's *hue* is usually the same as its name, like red, orange, yellow, green, blue, and violet.

Saturation refers to the vibrancy or intensity of the hue. Pure saturated colors have names like fire engine red, lemon yellow, or royal blue.

Saturated colors are often bright.

If you add white to a hue, it becomes a paler version of the original, called a *tint*. Often these colors are pastels—baby blue, sherbet green, or pink. Adding black to a hue results in a darker, often duller color. These colors are known as *shades*. Both tints and shades are lower saturation colors. Burgundy red, old gold, and hunter green are examples of shades. If you add gray to a hue you get a *tone*, which is usually a more subtle version of the color you started out with.

Pastel tints

Shades usually read as dark.

Tones have a gray cast.

The *temperature* of a color is whether it reads as cool or warm. If you look at a color wheel with yellow at the top, generally the colors on the left side of the wheel—green, blue, and violet—are known as cool colors and the colors on the right side—red, orange, and yellow—are known as warm colors. Cool colors are usually more serene and calm, like water or sky. Warm colors are often more active and energetic, like fire or sunlight.

For the purpose of creating quilts, *value* is perhaps the most important characteristic of color.

Value refers to whether a color is light, medium, or dark. Value is crucial in establishing shapes and lines in quilting. If you want a shape to show up, it needs to be bordered or surrounded by a different color or value.

Quilters tend to buy a lot of medium value fabrics and fewer lights and darks. I have been guilty of this myself. For a very long time, I rarely included white or light values in my work.

Value is relative. Some medium fabrics, for example, read as light when placed next to a dark value fabric but read as dark when placed next to a light value.

In *Beach Glass* I used several light values to surround the colorful Improv blocks. All of them look light compared to the blocks, but some look medium to dark when placed next to the lightest value.

Beach Glass by Cindy Grisdela, 27˝ × 32˝, 2017
Value is relative to its surrounding colors.

The most successful quilts use a range of values from light to dark.

Kaleidoscope has mostly medium values, but the design is defined by the light backgrounds and the dark arcs. I didn't plan it, but once I put the pieces together, I saw the bright white triangles forming a star like shape around the central block, because the background of the confetti units is a light silver. The subtle value change from bright white to silver created an interesting secondary design.

Kaleidoscope by Cindy Grisdela, 57″ × 57″, 2018
Subtle value changes create secondary design.

Partly Sunny illustrates the importance of value. A range of gray values from light to dark forms the base of the composition in the Improv Curves and Angled Stripes. That base gives the bright colors room to pop and move the eye around the design.

When you're evaluating the values in your composition, try taking a photo and viewing it in black-and-white. Taking the color out of the equation helps you to see if your values are distributed the way you want them.

Partly Sunny by Cindy Grisdela, 32″ × 32″, 2018
Improv Curves and Angled Stripes create vibrant design.

Color Palettes

I have a few favorite color recipes that I go back to again and again when I'm starting a new quilt. For me, color is almost always the starting point in any design. I want to see how different colors interact in the composition.

There are many other color combinations out there, and if you search "color schemes" on the internet, you'll find them. But these are the ones I find the most useful to give me a place to begin, even if I invariably make changes as I go along. I created several small quilt tops to illustrate the different color recipes, so it would be easier to see the changes.

MONOCHROMATIC

In some ways a monochromatic color palette is the easiest to use, because you just need lights, mediums, and darks in one color family, in this case blue. Value is essential here, because the contrast between the values is all you have to define your lines and shapes. I like to use as many different tints, tones, and shades of the color family as I can, pushing the blues almost to green on one side of the color wheel and almost to purple on the other side. This type of color palette can be very soothing to the eye, but it risks being boring.

A monochromatic color recipe with a variety of blues

ANALOGOUS

Analogous colors are two or more colors that are next to each other on the color wheel. In my example, I've used green, blue, and purple, but warmer colors like yellow, orange, and red would also be considered analogous, or any other groupings that touch each other on the color wheel. This color palette is often more engaging than a monochromatic palette, since you have more colors and values to work with. I chose to emphasize the blues and purples in the design and added just a couple of greens for accent. For another example of an analogous color palette, see also *Blue Maze* (pages 32 and 34).

An analogous color palette of blue and purple with green for contrast

TRIADIC

Triadic colors are those that are evenly spaced around the color wheel. The most obvious example would be the primary colors—red, yellow, and blue. I've chosen to use red-violet, orange, and green in my example. This palette is usually energetic without being jarring. You can tone it down by using less saturated colors, and by choosing one or two of the colors as dominant and the other as an accent. For another example of a triadic color palette, see also *Red Rover* (pages 9, 38, and 46).

Triadic colors form a triangle on the color wheel, like red-violet, orange, and green.

COMPLEMENTARY

Complementary colors are the most active and vibrant of the palettes I've introduced. They are opposite each other on the color wheel and tend to bounce off one another in an eye-popping way if you use them in equal amounts in your design. Examples of complementary pairs are red and green, orange and blue, and yellow and purple. The way to tame a complementary color palette is to choose one color as the primary color and use the other sparingly. I've made that choice with the orange accent in my mostly blue example. For another way to handle a double-complementary color palette, see *Window Dressing* (page 35).

Complementary color scheme with blue dominant

ANYTHING GOES

Of course, you can use all the colors if you want to. What I call the Anything Goes color recipe is a lot of fun, but can be chaotic if you don't take steps to calm things down. In *Under the Big Top*, I used curved strip interior borders in a deep purple and white to give the eye a place to rest in an otherwise extremely busy composition. Small blocks with white backgrounds placed in a diagonal line in the central design also help to inject some space into the riot of color.

PUT THE THEORY INTO PRACTICE

So how do you put these theories into practice?

First decide on the mood you want to convey in your quilt. Monochromatic and analogous palettes tend to be more peaceful and harmonious, especially if you use cool colors like green, blue, and purple. If you're aiming for a more cheerful, energetic feeling, a triadic or complementary scheme may be appropriate with warmer colors like red, orange, and yellow. An Anything Goes choice often has an exuberant, childlike feel. Or a range of neutrals may also be a good choice if you want a low-volume design.

Under the Big Top by Cindy Grisdela, 26″ × 28″, 2019

An Anything Goes color recipe with calming light areas

I recommend starting out with 8–12 fabrics for a new quilt. Of these, 6–8 fabrics reflect the warm or cool mood you've chosen. The amount of fabric needed depends on the size of your quilt. Remember to include a variety of values—lights, mediums, and darks—in your chosen colors.

CONSIDER THE DULLS

Consider including 1 or 2 fabrics that are less saturated, even dull, if your composition is on the warm side, or more saturated and brighter if your design is more muted. Dull values are often considered "uglies" because of their muddier appearance, but using dulls sparingly can give the brighter more saturated colors room to shine.

ADD THE SPARK

You're almost there! Choose 1 or 2 fabrics that are a different color or a different value than your basic color choices. I call this "adding the spark," and it adds just a bit of unpredictability to your design that can make all the difference in creating a successful quilt. The spark may be a complementary color, or a darker or lighter value, than your other fabrics. Experiment with several different choices to see which one creates the "wow" factor. Once you have your fabrics picked out, lay them out on the table and take a picture, then view it in black-and-white to help you see if you have a good range of values.

Let's look at the fabrics in *Balloon Fiesta* as an example.

Balloon Fiesta by Cindy Grisdela, 19″ × 27″, 2018

A warm color palette is more interesting with dull gold plus purple and green for contrast.

For this quilt I chose a warm color palette of red, orange, and yellow. I pushed the red out to pink and added a medium orange and a lighter orange. Then I added the gold you see in the improv curves and the upper border for my dull value.

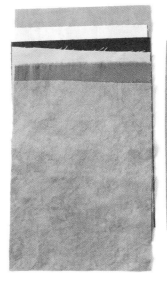

Adding a dull value can help the other colors shine.

For my sparks, I chose a purple in a much darker value than the rest, and a different color in the lime green. The composition is much more interesting with those additions to the basic warm color scheme than it would have been without them.

Adding contrasting colors can make a design more compelling.

Blue Maze by Cindy Grisdela, 27″ × 32″, 2019

Black lines create a maze-like structure for angled stripes and Improv curves.

Combining Palettes

You don't have to limit yourself to just one color palette in your designs. Often, I use a combination of color schemes. Compare *Blue Maze* with its straight analogous color palette of blues and purples with *Jewel Box*, which has sparks of orange and lime green. Another example is *Radiance* (pages 15, 22, and 46). The warm Improv blocks in the center of the composition appear to glow against the background of cool blues, greens, and purples.

Jewel Box by Cindy Grisdela, 25″ × 35″, 2015

Sparks of orange and lime green enliven this design.

Journey Home by Cindy Grisdela, 30″ × 48″, 2016

Improv blocks on an asymmetric background

Journey Home uses three color ideas in combination. The three focal blocks are mostly analogous, the blocks in combination are complementary, and the blue background has three different values in a monochromatic arrangement to add interest to the negative space.

This process also works in a neutral palette. *Neapolitan* uses a range of values in brown, dull pink, taupe, and cream, with pops of turquoise for the spark.

Learn to trust your instincts about color. There are no hard-and-fast rules, just suggestions for a starting point to come up with your own personal color vocabulary. If you want to explore these color ideas further without committing to a full quilt, consider choosing one composition like I did and make different small quilt tops using the various color options. You can turn them into pillows, or sew them together into one larger quilt, but you will have learned a good deal about the color theory with a relatively small amount of effort. Each of my color examples is 17″ square.

Neapolitan by Cindy Grisdela, 27″ × 36″, 2020

A change of pace with neutral fabrics, plus a spark of bright turquoise

elements and principles
OF DESIGN

Blue Maze by Cindy Grisdela, 27″ × 32″, 2019

Since there are no patterns to follow in Improv, you have to have another way to establish good design. Artists of all mediums use basic design principles to help organize their compositions, and these can apply to artistic quilt designs too. There are two components of artistic design—the elements of design are the building blocks of your composition, and the principles of design are the concepts you use to arrange those elements.

If you look these concepts up on the internet, you will find varying lists of elements and principles of design. These are the ones I find most relevant to creating art quilts. Remember these are not iron clad rules you have to follow, but rather a set of organizing ideas that may be useful in evaluating your designs.

Elements of Design

LINE

Line is one of the most basic elements of art. Along with color, lines are often the first thing you see when you look at a quilt. Lines can be thick or thin, straight or curved, zigzag or diagonal. Lines can be elements on their own, or they can define a shape. Lines provide a path for the eye to follow, so it's important to make sure that your lines move the eye around the composition effectively, rather than shooting out of the space you've created.

In *Window Dressing*, lines are the focus of the design. Horizontal lines imply a landscape, or an architectural shape. The stitching lines create energy, activating the large areas of negative space. And the angled lines in the focal Improv block imply depth.

Window Dressing by Cindy Grisdela, 18″ × 35″, 2016
A composition of simple lines and one shape.

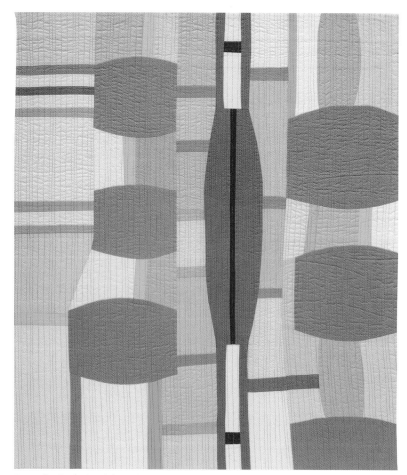

Transit by Cindy Grisdela, 27˝ × 32˝, 2018

Lines help to define shapes and activate a background.

In *Transit*, curved lines convey the neutral shapes, while a combination of vertical and horizontal lines in low saturation tints define the background space.

Diagonal lines add energy to the composition of *Aquarius*. The central pod shape is composed of diagonal lines going from left to right and the curved diagonals of blue appear to flow underneath the pod suggesting water or air.

Aquarius by Cindy Grisdela, 47˝ × 53˝, 2018

Diagonal lines are often the most dynamic lines.

SHAPE

Shapes are defined by lines that connect with each other. Straight lines describe regular shapes such as squares or rectangles, while curved lines describe circles or waves. Shapes can be hard-edged and geometric or soft-edged and organic.

The shape of *Flying Saucer* (below) is determined by softly curving brown lines. I established the interior shapes as the focus of the design by choosing medium shades to contrast with the darker lines and the lighter background.

Don't forget the negative space. Your lines should fall so that the background (negative) shapes are as interesting as the positive shapes of the design.

Flying Saucer by Cindy Grisdela, 12″ × 12″, 2019
Shapes are defined by lines that connect.

COLOR

Color is defined by hue, temperature, saturation, and value. It's often the first impression we have of a design. Color is such an important element of design that it gets its own chapter. (See Choosing a Color Palette, page 23.)

TEXTURE

Texture is how the surface looks to the viewer—rough or smooth, silky or grainy, waxy or mottled. In quilting, you have the opportunity to create texture through the fabrics that you use, the stitching that you add, and the surface design techniques you apply.

Autumn Curves has a rich texture because of the combination of patterned fabrics with solids in the design. The multiple curved blocks also add interesting visual texture that keeps the eye moving around the design.

Autumn Curves by Cindy Grisdela, 32″ × 32″, 2019
Texture can be created by fabric, stitching, or surface design.

With primarily solid fabric quilts, you can also create texture through the stitching lines. The texture in *Color Weave* comes from the various motifs in different areas of the quilt, including spirals, fans, pebbles, straight stippling, and seashells.

Color Weave by Cindy Grisdela, 18″ × 24″, 2019
Dynamic diagonal lines plus texture in stitching

Photo by Gregory R. Staley

Principles of Design

BALANCE

The elements of your design have visual weight in terms of shape, color, and texture. You need to balance that visual weight to create an effective composition. Designs that are symmetrically balanced have the same weight on both sides. *Seashells* has a visual line down the center both horizontally and vertically, and the design is the same on both sides.

Most of my designs are asymmetrical, because that aesthetic appeals to me more, but there's no right or wrong way to achieve design balance. It's part of your quilting DNA to prefer one or the other.

Red Rover is asymmetrically balanced with most of the visual weight in the Angled Stripe border on the left and bottom edges. The interior Curved Strip borders lighten up the weight and the stripe block in the upper right corner helps to balance the whole, even though it is small relative to the rest of the composition.

Seashells by Cindy Grisdela, 18˝ × 36˝, 2009

Symmetrical balance is often more restful.

Photo by Gregory R. Staley

Red Rover by Cindy Grisdela, 29˝ × 37˝, 2020

An asymmetrically balanced design with visual weight in one area balanced by elements in another area

FOCUS

The focal point of a design is the area that you want to emphasize to viewers. It can be a shape, line, color, or texture. Not every design needs a focal point, but many compositions have them. Where should it go? Generally, it's better not to have the emphasis dead center in the design. There's an artistic term known as *the rule of thirds* that's helpful in deciding where your focal point should be.

Divide your composition into three rows and three columns. The intersection of one of those lines is where the focal point should go.

Happy Days has its focal point just to the left of center, while the focal point of *Nautilus* is in the upper left. *Window Dressing* (page 35) has its focal point in the upper right.

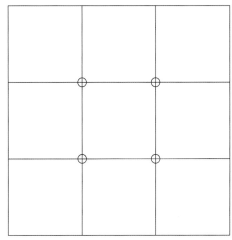

The rule of thirds is a useful idea to help you place a focal point.

Happy Days by Cindy Grisdela, 27″ × 27″, 2018

A focal point can be a block or shape.

There Are Exceptions

OF COURSE, *BLUE CONFETTI* (PAGES 12, 48, 49, AND 67) AND *KALEIDOSCOPE* (PAGE 27) BOTH BREAK THIS CONVENTION BY HAVING THE FOCAL POINT RIGHT IN THE CENTER. USE THESE CONCEPTS AS GUIDELINES, NOT AS RULES THAT CAN'T BE BROKEN.

Nautilus by Cindy Grisdela, 23″ × 34″, 2016

Focal block set asymmetrically on a neutral background

REPETITION

Repetition generates rhythm, which creates movement and makes the design more appealing to the viewer. You can repeat colors, lines, block units, or any other elements to achieve this effect.

Look at *Happy Days* (pages 11 and 39) again. The blocks form a repetitive pattern that helps move the eye around the design. Strategic grouping of the blocks with white in them to the left of center produces a rhythm that forms a secondary shape in the design, adding to the visual appeal.

The concept of repetition is important in *Partly Sunny* too. Both the Improv Curves and Angled Stripes are repetitive elements by themselves, but the strips of color add an additional layer of rhythm and movement. In addition, notice the medium gray vertical stripes. They are deliberately placed to help move the eye around the composition.

VARIETY

Variety is closely related to repetition. If you repeat the same blocks over and over, you have achieved repetition, but your design can become static. To generate a more dynamic design, consider varying the elements in some way.

Neapolitan has variety in the types of units in the design—Improv Curves, Angled Stripes, and Improv blocks—as well as in the colors used to create those elements. The colors are controlled, but the design varies the saturation levels of those colors. The lighter Angled Stripe blocks appear as shadows of the darker ones.

Partly Sunny by Cindy Grisdela, 32″ × 32″, 2018

Repetition creates movement.

Neapolitan by Cindy Grisdela, 27″ × 36″, 2020

Variety in the blocks and colors used can be effective against a static design.

Jewel Box uses the same Improv Curve shape but varies the size and color of the units. It would be a much less lively design without that variation. The analogous green/blue/purple color palette is enhanced with pops of yellow/orange/red in the smaller curved units.

Jewel Box by Cindy Grisdela, 25″ × 35″, 2015

Achieve variety in similar blocks by making them different sizes.

UNITY

Unity results in harmony. In a unified design, all of the elements and principles are working together to create a harmonious whole. It feels complete, like nothing needs to be added or taken away.

Aquarius is a unified composition with a clear focal point and energetic lines. The curved lines are repetitive and there is variety in the size and color of the shapes. The diagonal flow of the blue shapes under the central pod shape also provides balance and depth.

Aquarius by Cindy Grisdela, 47″ × 53″, 2018

An example of unified design with a focal point

Neon Fizz by Cindy Grisdela, 32˝ × 32˝, 2019

Unified design without a focal point

Neon Fizz is a good example of a unified design without a clear focal point. The diagonal line created by the two small Improv curve units directs the eye into the composition, while the curved lines and the different values in the color palette provide repetition and variety. The black stripes add an unexpected surprise for the viewer.

Using Design Principles in Improv

As you are creating, it's helpful to keep these elements and principles in mind. Once your design is finished, step away from it for at least a day and then come back and evaluate it with fresh eyes. Below are some questions to ask before you sew everything together or before you quilt it.

Are my lines and shapes dynamic? Have I placed my lines so the negative space also describes an interesting shape? Do the shapes and lines move the eye around the design successfully? (See Elements of Design, page 35.)

Is my color palette clear and does it enhance the composition? (See Choosing a Color Palette, page 23.)

Is there visual balance in the design, either symmetric or asymmetric? Have I looked at a black-and-white picture to make sure my values are reading well without heavy areas that drag the composition down? (See Principles of Design, page 38.)

If I have a focal point, is it clear what it is? If I don't have a focal point, do I need one? Could I group some colors or shapes to direct the eye more effectively? (See Focus, page 39.)

Do I have repetition of colors and shapes? Have I created an interesting rhythm to move the eye successfully around the design, or is there a spot that stops the eye or directs it outside the frame? (See Repetition, page 40.)

Is there variety in the color, shape, and line? Have I created a lively balance among my elements, or is there too much sameness that feels static? (See Variety, page 40.)

Does the design feel complete, or is there something missing? (See Unity, page 41.)

Is my design predictable, or have I created some element of surprise for the viewer? Have I added the spark in my color palette? Have I provided an unexpected line or shape? Have I given some areas of calm if my composition is busy? (See Choosing a Color Palette, page 23.)

anatomy of improv:
THREE WAYS TO CREATE IMPROVISATIONALLY

Neapolitan by Cindy Grisdela, 27″ × 36″, 2020

mprov design has been around as long as people have been making scrap quilts, and there are many different ways to work without a pattern. Some of them may feel familiar, like making a variety of different blocks and arranging them into a pleasing design, or sewing strip sets and cutting them up to create interesting lines and shapes. Others may be less comfortable, like cutting shapes out freehand with a rotary cutter.

Improv design is a process. Not having a pattern to follow makes things both easier and harder. Harder of course because there's no direction on what to do next, but also more freeing as an artist because you get to decide what goes where.

Let's look at three ways to create improvisationally.

One Repeating Unit

The unit can be as simple or as complex as you like. A half-square triangle is fairly simple, while a multiple-cut curve block is a little more complex.

Red Pennants uses one simple block—a rectangle with a half-square triangle on one corner. The design works because of changes in the colors used in each block and in the orientation of the blocks. You could also vary the angle of the triangle shapes to add energy to the composition.

Rectangle block with a triangle in one corner

Red Pennants by Cindy Grisdela, 12″ × 12″, 2018

A simple block repeated in different colors and orientations

Seashells is a more complex design, with multiple-cut curves in a variety of soft batiks. The curved block isn't difficult to make, and it results in interesting lines and shapes when you use a variety of fabrics. (See Easy Multiple-Cut Curves, page 50.)

Seashells by Cindy Grisdela, 18˝ × 36˝, 2009

A more complex block results in an engaging interplay of lines and shapes.

Photo by Gregory R. Staley

A single block with multiple-cut curves

You can also create a striking Improv quilt design with just one block. *Nautilus* features one oversized Improv block in soft yellows and grays, with a pop of pink and lime green. The block is set asymmetrically on a plain taupe background, and the background is activated by the inclusion of rectangles in two different but related colors.

A minimalist design like this is simple but challenging to get right. Getting an interesting balance between the positive space (the Improv block) and the negative space in the background is essential. The rectangles in different values in the background help to make the lines and shapes of the negative space appealing.

Nautilus by Cindy Grisdela, 23˝ × 34˝, 2016

A minimalist design with just one block

Red Rover by Cindy Grisdela, 29″ × 37″, 2020

A triadic color palette and dynamic lines energize the block units.

Multiple Block Units

Many Improv quilts are created using multiple block units, such as Improv Log Cabin–style blocks, curved blocks, stripes, inserts, or a combination of these.

Red Rover and *Radiance* are two examples of using the same multiple block units for different effects.

Red Rover uses a mostly triadic color palette of orange, purple, and green with a combination of Angled Stripe blocks and Improv blocks in the center design. Asymmetrical borders of Curved Strips and Angled Stripes complete the composition. It's a lively composition due to the color choices and the angled lines that provide energy.

Using multiple blocks in combination is a popular way to create Improv quilt designs.

In contrast, *Radiance* is a more subdued design with a base of cool blues and purples. The warm reds and oranges in the center design provide the spark that makes the composition more striking. In this layout, the center is composed of only Improv blocks and the Curved Strips and Angled Stripes make up the asymmetrical borders.

Radiance by Cindy Grisdela, 15″ × 20″, 2018

Warm contrasting blocks seem to glow.

New Day is a medley of units—Improv blocks, Improv Curves, stripes, and insets in a joyous colorful composition. I made the units mostly in multiples of three so they would fit together like a puzzle, adding coping strips where needed to make it all work.

New Day by Cindy Grisdela, 12″ × 24″, 2018
Cheerful variety of blocks
Photo by Gregory R. Staley

USING COPING STRIPS

When you're designing improvisationally with multiple units, sometimes you need to add a strip, block, or section to make everything fit when you sew the design together. I call these "coping strips" and they're a way to turn a potential mistake into a design element.

In *Partly Sunny*, I combined Improv Curve units with Angled Stripes to create the composition. The Angled Stripe units (page 63) are designed with different values of gray, plus a pop of color. I made those units at different times, and the ones with purple in them turned out to be slightly smaller than the rest. I could have cut them all down to the same size, but I used the opportunity to add an unexpected element. Each of those blocks has a vertical gray stripe added to the horizontal unit to make the block the correct size. The vertical stripes are carefully distributed to move the eye around the composition.

I used a similar coping mechanism in *Neon Fizz* (pages 19 and 42). Some of the Improv curved blocks turned out smaller than the rest, so I added black strips to one side of those blocks to compensate, turning a mistake into a design opportunity.

For more details on other ways to use coping units, see Controlled Log Cabin Puzzle–Style (page 57).

These are the units I design with most often, but there are many others available to you. There is no limit to the original designs you can make this way if you let your imagination run free.

Partly Sunny by Cindy Grisdela, 32″ × 32″, 2018

Gray vertical stripes turn a mistake into a design feature.

Free Cutting and Sewing

The first two ways of creating Improv quilts are relatively easy, since they're similar to the block-based format of more traditional quilts.

Creating with free cutting and sewing is a little more challenging, but it's a fun way to design with a little practice.

Think of your rotary cutter as a drawing tool, and use it to draw freehand curves, for example. It takes some practice to get comfortable with this technique and draw the lines the way you see them in your head, but it's well worth the effort.

These quilts are designed on the design wall before any sewing is done. The design process is improvisational, but the construction needs to be precise in order to have the lines and shapes fall where you want them to.

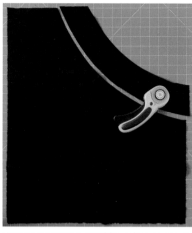

Use your rotary cutter like a drawing tool to cut curves freehand.

Blue Confetti, *Aquarius*, and *Kaleidoscope* (page 27) were all designed using freehand curves cut with a rotary cutter, without using templates or marking.

Blue Confetti by Cindy Grisdela, 42˝ × 44˝, 2019

Freehand arcs and spines define a contemporary Bulls Eye quilt.

Aquarius by Cindy Grisdela, 47˝ × 53˝, 2018

Freehand curves in an abstract composition.

In the following guided technique exercises, you'll get details on how to create improvisationally in each of these three ways.

techniques and GUIDED EXERCISES

Blue Confetti by Cindy Grisdela, 46″ × 47″, 2019

Easy Multiple-Cut Curves

Improv Curves are popular techniques that look more complicated than they are. Start out with squares that are larger than you want your finished block to be and cut the curves freehand with your rotary cutter—there's no need for patterns or templates. The blocks are squared up after they are sewn. This is a good exercise to practice using your rotary cutter like a drawing tool.

Blocks that have just one curved cut are modern versions of the traditional Drunkard's Path pattern. In the traditional version, the curved seams match to create a circle. In my Improv version, the curved seams don't match, giving the block a fun wonky edge.

Creating Improv Curve blocks with multiple cuts gives you more lines and shapes to play with in your design, and it's just as easy as making blocks with just one curved cut. With no pins, no templates, and large blocks to square up at the end, you'll be confident with curves in no time.

These blocks are a great choice to create Improv designs using just one, or mainly one, block in different colors and orientations. See *Playing with Colors* (next page and page 23), *Seashells* (pages 38 and 45), and *Retro Circles* (page 54).

GENTLE CURVE CUTS

Cut the curves in a gentle upward arc and try to avoid a downward "hook" at the end of your cut. The upward arcs are easier to sew together.

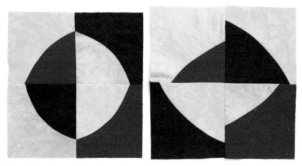

Traditional Drunkard's Path block (*left*) compared with Improv version (*right*)

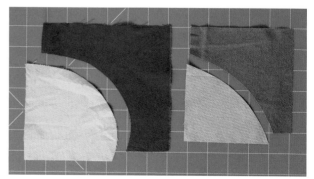

Cut with a gentle upward arc (*right*) and avoid a hook (*left*).

Playing with Colors by Cindy Grisdela, 45″ × 54″, 2008

Color wheel quilt using one multiple-cut curved block in different colors and placements.

Sew all seams with a ¼″ seam allowance, and then press the seams toward the smallest arc.

1. Choose 4 fabrics in one color family. In this example, I'm using red batiks. Cut 1 square 6½″ × 6½″ from each fabric.

2. Stack the 4 squares with the edges even, right side up. You will be making 3 cuts in the stack—one fewer than the number of fabrics you have.

Cut Blocks Larger

CUT YOUR SQUARES AT LEAST 2″ LARGER THAN YOU WANT THE SEWN BLOCK TO BE. TO ENSURE YOU HAVE ONE OF EACH OF YOUR FABRICS IN EACH BLOCK, MAKE ONE LESS CUT THAN YOU HAVE FABRICS. FOR EXAMPLE, IF YOU'RE USING 4 FABRICS YOU WILL MAKE 3 CUTS.

3. Use your rotary cutter to cut a gentle curve through all 4 layers. I usually start in the lower left and cut from the bottom of the stack to the left side, creating an arc that looks a little like a slice of pizza.

First curved cut

4. Moving right, cut 2 more gentle curves in the squares. Aim for a variety of widths in each cut and don't make the curve too severe or it will be harder to sew together.

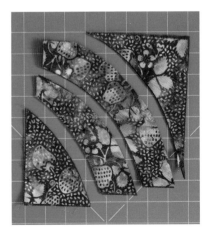

With 4 fabrics, make 3 curved cuts.

5. Shuffle the blocks to put one of each fabric in each block. Leave the leftmost arc, the pizza slice, where it is. In the next arc to the right, move the top fabric to the bottom. Move the top 2 fabrics in the next stack to the right to the bottom, and the top 3 fabrics in the final stack to the bottom.

Shuffle the block to get 4 different fabrics in each block.

There should be a different fabric in each curve of the block.

6. To sew the blocks together, label the stacks A–D.

7. Chain piece each A curve to each B curve, keeping them in order. There's no need to use pins, just start with the pizza slice on the bottom and sew slowly, gently easing the larger curve along. The edges will not match.

Overlap ¼″

WITH THE PIZZA SLICE ARC ON THE BOTTOM, POSITION THE TOP CURVE OVERLAPPING THE BOTTOM PIECE BY ABOUT ¼″ BEFORE SEWING THE SEAM. THIS WILL ENSURE THAT THE RAGGED EDGES OR "EARS" THAT RESULT FROM SEWING THE SEAM ALLOWANCES WILL BE EVENLY DISTRIBUTED ON EITHER SIDE OF THE BLOCK.

Overlap the top curve by ¼″ to ensure the "ears" of excess fabric are evenly distributed.

8. Add the C curve to the units you just created, and then add the D curves to complete the block.

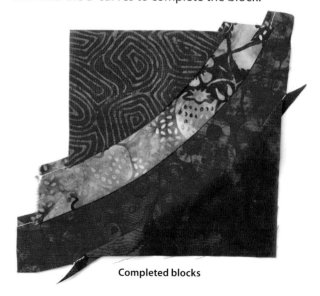

Completed blocks

Thread Jumper

USE A FOLDED PIECE OF SCRAP FABRIC ABOUT 1½″ × 3″ AS A "THREAD JUMPER" WHEN YOU ARE CHAIN PIECING. WHEN YOU FINISH THE SEAMS, PLACE THE THREAD JUMPER UNDER THE PRESSER FOOT AND SEW OVER IT, THEN CLIP THE CHAIN YOU WERE WORKING ON AND PROCEED. THIS TECHNIQUE AVOIDS HAVING TO PULL THE THREADS OUT AND CLIP THEM EVERY TIME, AND HELPS TO AVOID UNSIGHTLY THREAD "NESTS" ON THE BACK OF YOUR PIECING.

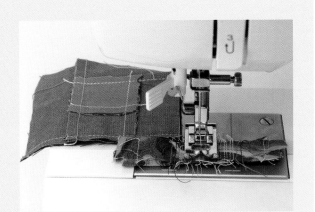

Use a thread jumper when chain piecing to save thread.

9. Square up the blocks to a uniform 5″. If your blocks are a slightly different size, that's okay—just make sure they are all trimmed to the same size.

To make the *Playing with Colors* quilt, you'll need 20 blocks in each of 6 different color families—red, orange, yellow, green, blue, and purple—120 blocks total.

10. Arrange the blocks in columns of 2 blocks each from warm red through cool purple. In my quilt, the blocks are alternated so the pizza arcs don't all meet in the center, creating more energy for the composition.

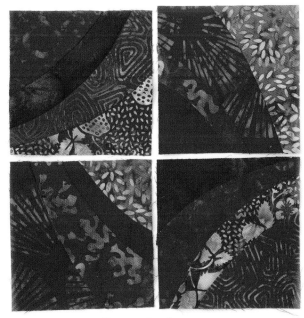

Alternate the pizza arcs.

Retro Circles by Cindy Grisdela, 28″ × 39″, 2018

Different look with different fabrics

ultiple-cut curves work with many different fabric combinations to create alternate looks. What if you use a combination of solids and low-volume prints? *Retro Circles* is made of 24 blocks: 4 blocks with 4 values of gray solids and 20 blocks with 2 gray value solids, 1 bright solid, and 1 low-volume black-and-white print.

1. Choose 4 fabrics for each set of blocks, such as medium gray, dark gray, hot pink, and a low-volume black-and-white print in this example.

2. Cut 8″ squares from each fabric. Stack them in a pleasing order with right side up.

3. Cut 3 gentle curves in the set.

Cut 3 gentle curves.

4. Label the curves 2A–D and shuffle the blocks. Leave the pizza slice alone, move the top fabric from the next curve to the right to the bottom, move the top 2 in the next stack to the bottom, and move the top 3 from the final stack to the bottom.

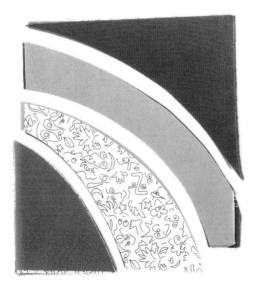

Shuffle the blocks.

5. Chain piece each A curve to each B curve, keeping them in order. Add the C curves to the units you just created, and then add the D curves to complete the blocks.

Completed curve units facing each other to form a circle

6. Square up the blocks to 6″.

7. Repeat for the remaining sets.

8. Arrange the blocks in 6 rows of 4 blocks each and sew together. You may choose to add a border or leave the composition as is.

ASK "WHAT IF?"

There are many different ways to cut and sew these blocks to create interesting Improv designs. What if you make the third cut so you create another pizza slice at the opposite end of the block?

Or what if you cut two pizza slices from opposite ends of the square?

Alternate third cut from an opposite side.

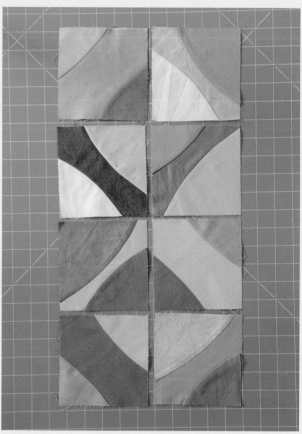

Two pizza cuts at opposite ends of the square

If you want to try these, cut your initial blocks about 3˝ larger than you want the sewn block to be, because the opposing curve often makes the block smaller.

What if you made the blocks oversized and cut some of them in half diagonally? These blocks started out about 20˝ square before cutting.

Sunny Side Up by Cindy Grisdela, 36˝ × 50˝, 2020
Oversized multiple-cut curve blocks with diagonal cuts

Use your imagination to come up with other ideas for multiple-cut curve blocks.

Controlled Log Cabin Puzzle-Style

Much of the time the blocks and units in my Improv quilts are fairly undisciplined. I like to use a lot of colors and I enjoy the random nature of the Improv process. But I'm always looking for new ways to express myself, and I began a new series asking, "What if my lines and shapes are more controlled?"

Start with a variety of Log Cabin blocks. I like 3˝, 6˝, 9˝, and 12˝ finished squares. To learn the techniques, it's fine to use scraps. Or you can work with a selected group of colors as I suggest in Choosing a Color Palette (page 23).

I recommend starting with the 3˝ blocks because you need more of them as a base, and then making a few 6˝ blocks and one or two larger blocks to anchor your design.

Start with Strips

IF YOU AREN'T STARTING WITH SCRAPS, IT'S HELPFUL TO CUT STRIPS FROM YOUR FABRICS SO YOU DON'T OVERTHINK YOUR CHOICES AS YOU DESIGN THE BLOCKS. CUT A 4˝ STRIP FROM EACH OF YOUR FABRICS. THEN IT WILL BE EASIER TO CUT THE STRIPS YOU NEED FOR YOUR BLOCKS. THE WIDTHS I USE THE MOST ARE 1˝, 1½˝, AND 2½˝. IT DOESN'T MATTER HOW LONG THEY ARE. YOU CAN USE A RULER OR JUST "EYEBALL IT" FOR A WONKIER LOOK.

Blue Puzzle GUIDED EXERCISE

Blue Puzzle by Cindy Grisdela, 23˝ × 23˝, 2020

Multiple block types put together like a puzzle.

These blocks are created Log Cabin–style with a center surrounded by "logs" (strips) of a different color or value. You can use any measurements you like inside the blocks as long as they finish to the correct size—3½˝, 6½˝, and 9½˝ including the seam allowances.

Sew all seams with a ¼˝ seam allowance, then press the seams away from the center. Here are some examples.

3˝ LOG CABIN BLOCKS

1. Cut a 1½˝ × 1½˝ center square.

3˝ block with a center and logs of a different color or value

2. Choose another fabric in a different color or value than your center for adding 1½˝ logs around the center block. Cut 1 log 1½˝ × 1½˝, 2 logs 1½˝ × 2½˝, and 1 log 1½˝ × 3½˝.

3. Sew the center and the 1½˝ log together first, and then add each 2½˝ log and then the 3½˝ log in a clockwise direction. The finished block should measure 3½˝ × 3½˝ square.

Sewn 3˝ block

Use Similar Colors

I RECOMMEND USING THE SAME OR VERY SIMILAR COLORS IN EACH ROUND OF MOST OF YOUR BLOCKS. THESE DESIGNS ARE VERY BUSY AND CAN END UP LOOKING CHAOTIC IF YOU HAVE TOO MUCH VARIETY IN THE BLOCKS THEMSELVES, ALTHOUGH A FEW BLOCKS THAT ARE DIFFERENT MAY ADD INTEREST.

3˝ block with multiple colors in the logs

3˝ block variations

4. Try different combinations to create more blocks:

2½˝ × 2½˝ center with 1˝-wide logs

1½˝ × 1½˝ center with a 1˝-wide log and another 1˝-wide log on the outside

2˝ × 2˝ center with 1¼˝-wide logs

The above measurements are cut sizes, including seam allowances.

Add Strips Without Cutting

TO SAVE TIME, YOU CAN ADD THE LOGS BY SEWING THE CENTER TO THE APPROPRIATE SIZE STRIP AND TRIMMING AS YOU GO, RATHER THAN CUTTING THE LOGS THE REQUIRED SIZES.

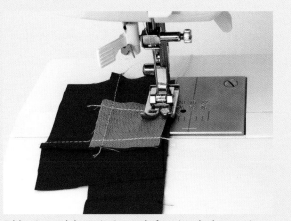

Add strips and then trim instead of cutting the logs to size.

6″ LOG CABIN BLOCKS

1. Cut a 2½″ × 2½″ center square.

2. Choose another fabric in a different color or value than your center, and cut and sew 1″-wide logs around the center block the same way you did to make the 3″ blocks.

3. Choose a third fabric in a different color or value than the other two, and cut and sew 2″-wide logs around the center. The finished block should be 6½″ × 6½″.

6″ block with a center and 2 rounds of logs
in different colors and values

4. Try different combinations to make more blocks:

2½″ center with 1″ and 2″ logs

2″ center with 1″, 1½″, and 1″ logs

3½″ Improv center with 2¼″ logs

The Step 4 measurements given are cut sizes, including seam allowances.

6″ block variations

What if you make some of your blocks with asymmetrical centers? The pink center of this block is a 1½″ square surrounded by 2 purple logs 1″ wide and 2 purple logs 1½ wide.

SIZE ADJUSTMENTS OF STRIPS OR BLOCKS

If your blocks end up smaller than you expected, either adjust your seam allowance or cut the outside strips ¼″ or so wider to accommodate. If your strips aren't quite long enough, it's fine to insert another fabric to make it the right size, as the block variations with the Improv center and the one with the red-orange outside logs illustrate (previous page). This is Improv after all, and sometimes that unexpected change in the routine is what gives the composition its personality.

9″ AND LARGER LOG CABIN BLOCKS

These bigger blocks are often the focal point of the design and there may only be a few of them, depending on the size of your quilt, so try to make them as interesting as possible. Consider using one of your 3½″ squares as the center and adding wider logs with insets.

1. Start with a 3½″ × 3½″ center square.

2. To make insets, select a 2½″-wide strip in a contrasting color or value from the center and cut a 3½″ rectangle from it.

3. Select a narrow strip, ¾″–1″ wide, of another contrasting color or value, and cut 2½″ rectangles from it.

4. Make cuts in your background rectangle to add the insets. Stitch the strip together, then stitch the inset unit to the center square.

5. Make 3 more inset units in the same way and stitch them to the center going clockwise. In this example, units 2 and 3 are both 2½″ × 6″ and unit 4 is 2½″ × 9½″.

Completed insets

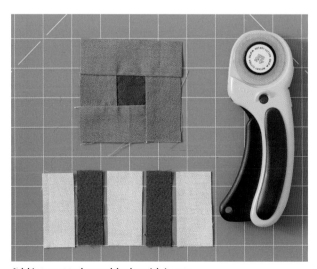

Add interest to larger blocks with insets.

6. If your block is smaller than 9½˝ at this point, add more logs until it reaches the correct size. This block was 7¼˝ square, so I added 1˝-wide logs of red-purple and 1¼˝-wide logs of a slightly different lime green to the outsides to make it the right size.

I deliberately set up my insets so they don't all touch the center square because it looks more interesting to me that way. You can decide whether you want your insets to touch the center or not, and if you want the insets on opposite sides of the center to be in line with each other or offset like mine are. There's a lot of flexibility. I decided to make the outermost round a lime green that is similar to the inset background to focus attention on that area. It would have a different look if the outermost log was another color entirely.

9˝ block completed with two additional rounds of logs

PUTTING IT TOGETHER

Once you have a variety of blocks to play with, it's time to arrange your design.

Start by laying out the larger anchor blocks. I don't like to put my focus block right in the middle of the composition. Usually it's slightly off center either to the right or left, up or down. That's because I think asymmetrical compositions are more interesting, but you can decide to put your focal point wherever it looks best to you. (See Focus, page 39.)

I put 2 of the 6˝ blocks touching the larger focal block, overlapping by about 3˝, and the third one floating in the upper right corner. You'll use your smaller blocks to fill in the blank spaces.

Using "coping" strips or units is another option to add interest to your design. I originally used the

Lay in the large anchor blocks first, then fill in with smaller blocks and units.

"coping" idea to refer to units that I added to make the blocks fit together—often stripes or units made from leftover scraps—but you can make use of the idea to add new lines and shapes to your composition even if they aren't strictly necessary.

Two of my favorite "coping" units are angled stripes and wonky triangles.

Angled Stripes

1. To create angled stripes to use as filler, cut about an 8˝ length from 6 of your 4˝ strips.

2. Stack the strips in a pleasing order. If your fabrics have a right and a wrong side, stack them for cutting *right side up*.

Rectangles for angled stripe coping units

3. Make 5 angled cuts the length of the strip to create 5 stacks. Make sure the angles vary in slant and width.

Make 4 angled cuts.

4. Shuffle the stacks to make stripes with different fabrics. From the leftmost stack, put the top fabric on the bottom.

5. Moving right, put the top 2 fabrics on the bottom of the next stack, then the top 3 fabrics to the bottom on the next stack and the top 4 fabrics on the next one. The stack on the far right stays as is.

Shuffled stripes

6. Take the top fabric from each stack, lay the stripe out next to your sewing machine to sew, and then move to the next layer down.

7. Sew the stripes right side together using a ¼˝ seam.

Sewn stripes

Larger Stripe Units

IF YOU WANT TO MAKE LARGER STRIPE UNITS, CUT LARGER RECT-ANGLES. I OFTEN USE 7˝ × 9˝ SIZE WITH 5–7 FABRICS AND MAKE ABOUT 5 ANGLED CUTS. THESE UNITS WILL CREATE 6½˝ BLOCKS THAT YOU CAN USE TO REPLACE SOME OF YOUR SMALLER BLOCKS IF YOU WANT TO. OR YOU CAN CUT 3½˝ × 6½˝ RECTANGLES.

Wonky Triangles

Wonky triangles are a fast way to add new lines and shapes to your design.

1. Cut rectangles from 2 fabrics that are either a different color or different values of the same color. You can make the triangles any size you want, but make sure the width of your rectangle is about double the height. I like to use 2½˝ × 5˝ rectangles.

2. Align the edges *right side up* and cut a rough triangle shape out of the center of the stacked rectangles. The angles don't have to be the same on each side.

Stacked rectangles with rough triangle shape cut through both layers.

3. Shuffle the triangle shape so you have 2 units.

4. Sew the triangle units right side together using a ¼˝ seam and trim to even the edges.

Sewn wonky triangles.

If you are careful about your blocks all being multiples of 3˝, you likely won't need the coping strips or blocks, but the idea is handy if some blocks don't work out exactly as you planned, or if you just want to spice up your design with something unexpected.

Blue Puzzle (pages 6 and 58) has a 9˝ focal block, 3 different 6˝ blocks, and a variety of 3˝ blocks, plus several angled stripe units and wonky triangles to add new lines and shapes. I added some resting space on 3 outer sides using dull blues.

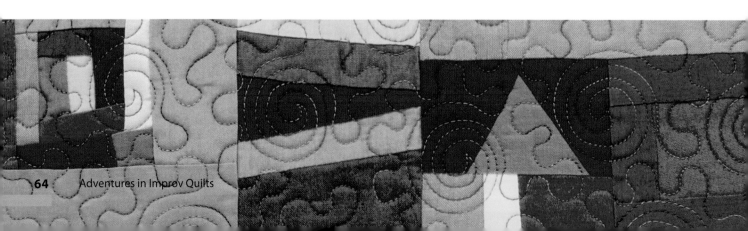

ASK "WHAT IF?"

What if you add curves to your composition?

New Day by Cindy Grisdela, 12″ × 24″, 2018

Add blocks with curves.

Photo by Gregory R. Staley

What if you make the angled stripes part of the composition instead of just a means of coping with fitting the design together?

Neapolitan by Cindy Grisdela, 27″ × 36″, 2020

Angled stripes are part of the composition instead of a coping mechanism.

These are just ideas to get you started. Use your creativity to think of more ways to combine these units to make exciting Improv quilts.

Freehand Curves

One of the things I enjoy most about Improv design is the fact that I never know when I start exactly what the quilt will look like when I'm finished. I like puzzles—crossword puzzles and jigsaw puzzles especially—and the Improv process feels a little like that to me.

Creating Improv quilts with freehand curves is a different process. Instead of creating independent blocks or units and arranging them on the wall to find a pleasing design, you lay in all the colors and make the design decisions before any seams are sewn. Although the sections can be sewn together as blocks, the quilt isn't designed that way.

In this method, you are really using fabric like paint to create your designs.

I still make two decisions to begin—how big and what colors. But I often take the time with these quilts to sketch out my initial design idea to use as a reference as I'm creating. I'm not a very good artist, so these sketches are quite rough and subject to change as I go. It doesn't matter what the sketch looks like as long as it serves as a reference for you.

If you are new to cutting freehand with your rotary cutter without using a template or ruler, I recommend taking a yard or so of fabric and just practicing. It can be any old fabric that you don't mind cutting up.

Cut an arc from one corner, and then cut curves based on that line in a variety of widths to get comfortable with the idea of using your rotary cutter like a drawing tool. Look at your curves with a critical eye. Is the width consistent, or if not does it look like it was meant to be that way?

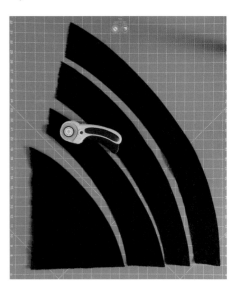

Practice freehand curves.

Blue Confetti by Cindy Grisdela, 42″ × 44″, 2019

Use freehand curves to design without templates or rulers.

Blue Confetti is the second in a series of quilts featuring freehand cut curves and arcs, accented with pops of color. The series is inspired by traditional Bull's-Eye quilts and it's a great exercise in large scale curves. I cut the arcs freehand, and then cut chunks of color to fill in the spaces within the spines. You can see in the images that the colors are just roughly laid in. It's definitely not a pretty process!

MAKING THE COMPONENTS

1. Decide on your colors using the tips in Choosing a Color Palette (page 23). In my sample, the large arcs are blue, the spines are dark gray, and the colors in the spines are mostly brights in an Anything Goes color recipe. The light areas are light silver. The quadrants started out about 24″ square.

2. Cut the central arcs in a variety of pie shapes so they don't all meet in the center and lay them out on the design wall.

3. Cut the long arcs freehand. You can decide how wide, how long, and how many they are. Lay them out either right next to or a short distance away from the central motif.

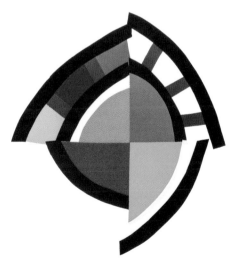

Begin cutting the arcs.

4. Cut the dark gray spines and lay them in between the arcs. My spines are cut 2½˝ to finish at 2˝.

5. Decide on the colors to fill in the spaces and cut rough shapes 1˝–2˝ larger on all sides than the openings. There is some "waste" in this process, but you can save the leftovers to make a great scrap quilt.

6. To make the "confetti pops," choose scraps of bright fabrics similar to those filling in the spines of your design. Cut squares or rectangles that are 1½˝ on one side and 1˝–2˝ on the other. They don't have to all be the same size.

Make confetti pops.

7. Cut 1½˝ strips from fabric that is the same or similar color to the arc fabric for the stems of the pops.

8. Cut 1½˝ strips from the light background fabric.

9. Cut the stems into random lengths and lay them out on top of the arc. Vary the distances between the pops slightly.

10. Cut 1½˝ squares from the background fabric strips and lay them on top of the stems, then add the color pops and another strip of the background fabric to complete the pop. The length of that strip will depend on the distance from the color pop to the next element in the design.

11. Once you're satisfied with the sequence, cut pieces of the light background 1˝–2˝ larger all around than the spaces between the pops and lay them underneath each pop in the arc.

When all of the elements are in place, I recommend taking several photos of the design, including one in black-and-white. As you're designing on the wall, it's easy to be too focused on one particular element or section and have trouble seeing the entire composition. Taking a photo of the whole piece helps to give the necessary distance to see potential problem areas before sewing everything together.

To evaluate the composition in terms of value, balance, repetition, and focus, refer to Elements and Principles of Design (page 34). Are your light and dark values reading the way you want them to? Is the design balanced, or are there light holes or dark areas that need to be adjusted? Do you have repetition of key elements and a variety in sizes and shapes?

After you've completed your evaluation, you're ready to sew.

Up to this point, you've designed improvisationally, cutting your elements freehand and arranging them on the wall, going with the flow. In contrast, the construction phase of the process has to be very specific if you want your lines and shapes to stay where you've put them.

Start with the smaller elements and work your way up to the larger sections.

ASSEMBLING THE QUILT TOP

1. Pin a spine rectangle to one of the backgrounds and transport the 2 pieces to the cutting table. The pieces should be right side up.

2. Use your rotary cutter to carefully cut along the edge of the spine section through both layers. I don't mark seam allowances in this process, so the finished piece will shrink naturally as it's sewn together.

3. Carefully flip the spine over so the 2 pieces are right sides together. Pin if necessary.

4. Sew with a ¼˝ seam. Press the seam to one side. Don't worry about the ends. It doesn't matter if they don't match because they will be trimmed later.

5. Sew the rest of the spines to their backgrounds to complete the unit. Remember to use the spine edge as the cutting line so the spine section will remain a rectangle.

6. To sew the spine section to one of the large curves, carefully pin the spine section to the curve right side up. I do this right on the design wall.

7. Transport the pinned unit to the cutting table and use your rotary cutter to cut along the line of the arc through all layers.

8. After cutting, you can use a chalk marker to put small hash marks on both edges to help you pin the 2 pieces together accurately if you wish.

9. Starting in the center, put the 2 pieces right sides together and pin along the edge, matching the hash marks if you used them.

10. Sew with a ¼˝ seam. Press the seam to one side.

11. Sew the pie shaped arcs in the center to their long pieced arcs in the same way, putting the pieces right sides together and pinning from the center out.

This process is the secret to get the confetti pops to stay in the curve you set up after sewing too. Start with the pops in the center of the arc and use the pop edge as the cutting line to add the pop to the background. Work your way from the center to the ends, adjusting the distance between the pops as necessary as you sew. You'll be glad you added a generous allowance on each side of the background chunks to make these adjustments without having to recut the background.

Add confetti pops to the adjacent arc.

Use the arc as a guide to cut the sewing line.

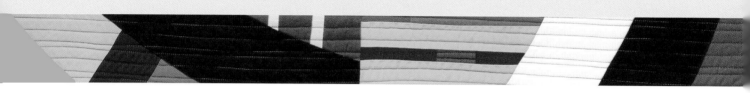

DON'T FEAR WASTING FABRIC

A word about the fear of wasting fabric. I struggled with this for a long time but was finally able to look at it another way. Fabric for an art quilter is what paint is to a painter. It's what we use to express ourselves. No one likes to waste material, but we're fortunate as fabric artists that our "waste" material can be saved to create something else later. Maybe it's better to think of them as "off cuts." I have a bin in my studio where all the scraps go and sometimes it's fun to dump them out and reimagine them into an entirely new composition.

The horizontal and vertical stripes in the center of *Blue Confetti* are an example of turning a problem into a design element. I sewed each quadrant of the design separately according to the steps outlined above, but one of them turned out smaller than the rest. I could have cut them all down to the same size, but I would have lost some elements that I liked, so I created stripes using the blue and silver, plus pops of aqua and pink. The design seemed more unified with the addition of this unexpected element.

Detail of *Blue Confetti* (full quilt, pages 12, 48, 49, and 67). Stripes add interest.

You can use these techniques to create many different designs.

Color Weave (at right and page 37) is a smaller version using arcs and spines.

Kaleidoscope (page 27) is a variation on this Bull's-Eye design. *Aquarius* (pages 36, 41, and 48) uses a similar arc and spine approach to create a different type of composition, while *Transit* (page 36) has gentle free-hand curves that define shapes.

Color Weave by Cindy Grisdela, 18″ × 24″, 2019

Bright colors with dark brown spines

Photo by Gregory R. Staley

Blooming (at right) is a new adaptation of the freehand curve concept, combining oversized curved shapes and large Improv blocks using both solid fabrics and printed batiks from Turtle Hand Batiks.

Blooming by Cindy Grisdela, 65″ × 65″, 2020

Oversized curves combine with large Improv blocks in another take on this design concept.

Photo by Gregory R. Staley

how do you know
IT'S FINISHED?

Finger Painting by Cindy Grisdela, 12″ × 12″, 2019

*S*ince there's no pattern to follow, sometimes it's hard to know when your composition is finished. Often there's a temptation to just sew it up and move on, and sometimes that is the right decision. But try to resist the temptation. If you want to be an artist, you have to learn to evaluate your work to improve it.

The first thing I do to evaluate a design is take plenty of photos during the process, both in color and in black-and-white.

Turn It Upside Down

Use the photos to turn the composition upside down or sideways. Just because you started the composition in one orientation doesn't mean that another way might not work better.

Partly Sunny (pages 27, 40, and 47) is a good example to consider. If you rotate the composition so that it's turned on its side, the design looks very different. It may not be better or worse, but it's worth checking out the options before you commit to one orientation or another.

Rotate the design to make sure you have the best composition.

Let It Marinate

This is a crucial step.

Recently I was working on a new composition that started out with just a few leftover blocks and an idea. I put them up on the design wall, added some more blocks and left them there for a few days. I knew something wasn't right about it, but I couldn't put my finger on what it was.

After reflecting on it, I realized that I needed to edit the colors. I had two different quilts going on and they weren't playing nicely together. I liked both the brown, red, white, and aqua curves and the colorful blocks and stripes, but they didn't belong in the same piece.

Beginning of an idea

Picasso's Chickens by Cindy Grisdela, 36″ × 40″, 2020

Photo by Gregory R. Staley

Restricting the colors to the brown, red, white, and aqua made all the difference. If I hadn't given the design time to marinate, I wouldn't have realized what the problem was and learned from it. Another lesson here is not to get too emotionally attached to the blocks and units that you make. If they don't go in this quilt, they can go in the next one and might be more successful. That's why the leftover basket is there.

You might ask why the center block still has some of the bright elements. I didn't forget about it! I made another block with the colors from the quilt and the entire design lost its energy. So I put the first one back. It provides a pop of color that is welcome because it's unexpected.

For questions to ask as you evaluate whether your design is finished or not, refer to Using Design Principles in Improv (page 42).

Trust Your Instincts

As you grow as an artist, it becomes more and more important to learn to trust your own instincts. It's fine to ask opinions of your spouse, your child, or your best friend, but you don't have to take their advice. Think carefully about whether the advice you are given lines up with your instincts about what your design may need.

Some people find it beneficial to join a critique group of other artists, and if you have that option available to you, it might be worth exploring. Just make sure that the group is geared toward constructive criticism.

As you are evaluating options on your design wall, really look at how each possibility affects you. You can toss out any option that results in a "That's okay" response. Keep the ones that cause your heartbeat to pick up a little bit and wait for the "Aha, that's it!" moment that says you have the right choice. Give yourself time and keep trying another fabric, another line, another shape until you get to that moment. Nobody can tell you what it is—you have to feel it.

After all, even if you want to enter a show or sell your work, you make art for yourself. Each of us has the ability to be creative and to express ourselves in fabric and thread in a unique way. No one else can create art in the same way you can. It's up to you to nurture that creative spark.

Blocks and tools for creating
Photo by Gregory R. Staley

add texture
WITH QUILTING

Metamorphosis by Cindy Grisdela, 12″ × 12″, 2017

Photo by Gregory R. Staley

*A*dding texture with the quilting stitches is a part of the quilt making process that I look forward to. That texture is one of the things that drew me to quilts in the first place, instead of becoming a painter or some other kind of artist. As quilt artists we have a unique ability to add another element of interest to our creations that simply isn't available to artists in other mediums.

One of the reasons I changed my artistic practice ten years ago to use mostly solids in my work instead of printed fabrics was so the texture of the stitching lines would show. I want the texture and dimension of the stitching lines to be just as important to the final composition as the lines and shapes I create in the fabric, rather than just a means to hold the three layers together.

With this in mind, it's important to ask yourself what you want to accomplish with your stitching. Sometimes dense free-motion stitching is the right choice to activate areas of negative space in the design. Other times irregularly spaced vertical or horizontal lines will be the best choice to complement a busy composition.

You don't need a special sewing machine for free-motion quilting, but you do need an open toe darning foot or a hopping foot so you can see where you're going, and the ability to lower the feed dogs. This eliminates any pressure on your quilt from the top or the bottom, so all the machine is doing is making the needle go up and down. This is what gives you the ability to move forward, backward, and sideways to create the stitches you want.

I did my free-motion stitching on a domestic BERNINA sewing machine for many years. Recently I've upgraded to a mid-arm BERNINA Q 20 that has a 20″ throat space so I can quilt larger quilts more easily. But I'm still moving the fabric to drive the stitches, rather than driving the needle, as you would do with a longarm machine.

Let's begin with the basics and work up to more complex ideas.

I piece with a BERNINA 440 machine and do free-motion stitching with a BERNINA Q 20.

Photo by Gregory R. Staley

Walking Foot

A walking foot attachment on your machine gives you a relatively painless way to add texture to your quilts, especially if the design has a lot going on. The advantage of a walking foot over a regular presser foot is the ability to feed the fabric evenly through on both the top and the bottom, which helps to minimize puckers or pleats on the back. But it's still a good idea to check the back periodically to make sure you don't have problems.

First decide if you want the lines to be vertical or horizontal. If there's a seam line to follow, use that. Otherwise mark the first stitching line with blue painter's tape or a chalk marker. If you choose to use a chalk marker, check it in an unobtrusive place before using, to make sure it will fully erase.

I start roughly in the middle of the piece, stitch the first line, and then stitch the lines to the left and right, using the edge of my walking foot on the previous stitching line as a guide. With my walking foot, the stitching lines end up about ½″ apart. I go over the entire top in this fashion, and then I go back and add another line of stitching in between some of the lines, but not all of them. This adds an irregular spacing that makes the texture more interesting to me.

Some quilters enjoy sewing lines even closer together in "matchstick" style, about ⅛″ apart. Try it on some smaller pieces to see what spacing appeals to you the most.

Detail of *Neon Fizz* (full quilt, pages 19 and 42) shows irregular spacing of lines.

Echoing Designs with Freehand Straight Lines

Another way to use straight lines to add texture is following the design lines and then echoing them. I discovered this almost by accident when I was quilting *Flying Saucer*. I quilted the motifs in the central area of the design and thought I would just use straight lines in the background. But then I asked, "What if?" and came up with a different idea. Stitching along the design lines created interesting texture when I pivoted and then echoed the stitching. I did this freehand with my hopping foot instead of using a walking foot because it was quicker, and I liked the flexibility. Some of the lines are more "organic" than straight, but I like the effect.

Flying Saucer by Cindy Grisdela, 12″ × 12″, 2019

Secondary pattern in stitching lines adds interest.

Combining Motifs in the Same Quilt

One of my favorite free-motion quilting techniques is combining different motifs in the same quilt. It's more interesting to stitch that way, and it's more interesting to look at once it's finished. I spent nearly ten years showing and selling my work at fine art and fine craft shows all over the country, and I wanted viewers of my work to be attracted to the lines and shapes of the composition initially, and then be drawn in to take a closer look by the texture of the stitching. I think about what motifs will go where when I'm designing the composition.

The concept works best if you have large areas of negative space to fill, as in *Wildflower Honey*, but it can also be effective to activate the space in smaller areas, like I did in *Aquarius* (pages 36, 41, and 48) and *Balloon Fiesta* (pages 18 and 31).

Wildflower Honey by Cindy Grisdela, 20˝ × 20˝, 2016
Different quilting motifs in different areas.
Photo by Gregory R. Staley

How do you decide which motifs to put where?

I have a grab bag of motifs that I like to use. I was originally a hand quilter when I started quilting many years ago, and it took me a while to get comfortable with free-motion machine stitching. I started out with a few motifs that I could execute fairly well, such as spirals and stippling, and then added new motifs as I gained confidence in my skills. I practiced on baby quilts, because babies don't care if your stitches are even—they just like the texture of the quilt.

Some motifs are well suited to allover designs, such as fans, nesting spirals, and the spiral and stipple combination, and some are good for borders and more linear spaces, such as square spirals, ribbon candy, and lollipop trees. Experiment with the motifs that appeal to you and be gentle with yourself. You'll get better with practice. Consider making smaller projects like as place mats, with a different motif or combination of motifs on each one, to practice while still making something useful.

NESTING SPIRALS

I use spirals frequently—open spirals, closed spirals, square spirals. Nesting spirals are a variation on a closed spiral that is a particular favorite. To stitch a closed spiral, first stitch a curve into the center, then pivot and come back out again without crossing any of your stitching lines. To make a closed spiral nest into its neighbor, when you come out of the center bring the stitching line close to another element—another stitching line or the edge of the piece—and pivot to echo back around to the opposite side of the curve. Do that one more time before starting a new spiral to create the nesting effect. This motif is good as a filler for a background or open space.

Nesting spirals

Detail of *Aquarius* (full quilt, pages 36, 41, and 48). Spirals appear to nest next to each other in an allover design.

SPIRAL WITH HOOK

Another spiral motif adds a hook on one side. Stitch your spiral into the center as you normally would, then come back out and stitch a hook shape before echoing the remainder of the spiral. Then pivot to stitch another spiral. The hook helps to fill in awkward spaces that sometimes happen in spiral motifs. It's another good background filler.

Spiral hook motif

Detail of *Sunny Side Up* (full quilt, page 57) with spiral hook motif

SQUARE STIPPLING

Most quilters are familiar with round stippling. It's one of the first motifs many of us learn. Square stippling is a bit more challenging, but it creates a nice texture. I like to think of it as designing building blocks, like the ones my sons played with when they were small. Start at an edge of your space and stitch a few stitches, then pivot and stitch in another direction for a few stitches. Repeat. It's important to make your pivots square. This motif has a mid-century modern feel and it's a good choice for filling an open space in your design, but you would need to scale up the size to make it work as a background filler.

I like to combine the square stipple with spirals for a different effect. Adding the curved element changes the direction of the stipples so they aren't as linear. One important thing to keep in mind as you're stitching is the fact that every time you change direction, you're creating a new texture. As you stitch, the batting is depressed along the lines of thread and pops up in the unquilted areas.

Square stippling with spirals

Detail of *Flying Saucer* (full quilt, pages 37 and 78), combining spiral with square stipple

FANS

Fans are fun to use on borders or rectangular interior spaces. Start at one edge of your space and stitch an arc. Pivot and stitch three or four stitches in a row, then pivot again to stitch a curve that echoes the arc. Repeat two or three times, then start another arc. Remember to stop a few stitches away from the next element. The stitching lines are not supposed to touch each other. Fans are a linear stacking motif stitched horizontally or vertically. When you get to the end of the row, start another arc that goes back in the opposite direction. Sometimes I throw in a spiral instead of the arc to add interest. Fans work in backgrounds, borders, and open spaces.

Fans

Detail of *Beach Glass* **(full quilt, page 26). Fans add a touch of whimsy.**

ECHOING SPIRALS

Stitch large spirals across the entire area you want to cover, and then go back and echo your stitching with lines about ⅛″–¼″ apart. There's more of a risk of puckers or bubbles with this motif because you have to leave large areas of unquilted space open for echoing. I usually use it on small pieces or in small areas of a quilt for this reason. The texture it creates is worth the risk though!

Echoing spirals

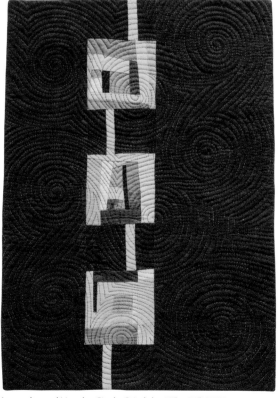

Lavender and Lime by Cindy Grisdela, 12″ × 17″, 2017
Echoing spirals work well on small quilts.

Graffiti-Style Quilting

Free-form quilting refers to methods of combining motifs in the same space in your quilt, graffiti style. It can work as an allover design, background filler, or in a small space. This style of stitching is a good way to elevate a simple composition to something truly spectacular. I do this in two ways—stacking motifs and free-form graffiti style.

STACKING MOTIFS

Divide your space into sections, either visually or using removable marks.

Stitch one motif area, and then move on to the next, for example:

• Nesting spirals

• Pebbles

• Small feather or paisley

• Spiral and stipple

Starry Night by Cindy Grisdela, 10″ × 20″, 2017
Stacking motifs elevate this simple composition.

In *Starry Night*, I created a simple composition of vertical lines in an analogous color palette, with a spark of lime green. I started with the lime green feather or paisley motif in the center. Normally I don't mark my free-motion stitching. I prefer to stitch the designs completely freehand. But in this case, I wanted to make sure that my paisley line was wavy, so I drew a light chalk line through the center where I wanted the stitching to go and stitched the motif along the line. On one side of the wavy paisley line I stitched a random series of pebbles, and then filled in the rest of the space with nesting spirals. On the other side, I used a spiral and stipple combination. The quilting makes the quilt more special than it would otherwise be.

Detail of *Starry Night*. A combination of nesting spirals, pebbles, paisley, and spiral and stipple in a stacking motif.

FREE-FORM STYLE

The completely free-form method is a bit more challenging to stitch, but well worth the effort. Choose 3–5 motifs that work well together:

• Spirals

• Seashells

• Pebbles

• Waves

• Peacock feather

Note that these are all curved, organic types of motifs, rather than linear ones. Many of my quilts use fairly linear lines and shapes and I like to offset that in the stitching with more organic forms.

You can start at an edge of your work or in the center. Stitch 3–5 spirals, for example, and then move to pebbles, seashells, or peacock feathers. I recommend grouping your motifs in odd-numbered sets when possible, except the pebbles, which can go wherever they are needed. Waves and pebbles are good filler motifs when you don't have room to stitch another spiral or larger motif.

Try to stay relaxed and don't worry if you stray off the intended path. If you stitch something you didn't intend to, if your pebbles are more oval than round for example, don't worry about it. Either ignore it or do it again so it becomes a design decision instead of a mistake. Remember that echoing is your friend. If you stitch a motif that you aren't happy with, try echoing it a few times to create a new texture. And if you end up boxed in a corner, you can echo your way out to get to a spot where you can go forward again.

Detail of *Nuance* (full quilt, next page). Choose 3–5 motifs that work together for a free-form stitching motif.

Free-form stitching

Listen to music if it relaxes you and try to take frequent breaks as you stitch. If you feel your shoulders creeping up to your ears, it's time to take a break. Watch your posture too. Your chair and your sewing table should be set so you can sit up straight with your hands at a 90° angle to your work and your feet flat on the floor. Tension in your body makes it harder to get even stitches.

For more information on free-motion quilting, see Resources (page 94).

Nuance by Cindy Grisdela, 12˝ × 45˝, 2017

Free-form stitching as allover texture on a neutral palette

TIPS TO REMEMBER

- It won't be perfect! Free-motion quilting is a hand-guided process, even though you're using a machine to make the stitches.

- If you feel like you've made a mistake, keep going. Either ignore it or do it again so it becomes a design element.

- Just think about creating *texture*—that's what people see when they see your stitching.

- Nobody knows what you meant to do—they just see the lovely result.

- Have fun!

Choosing Batting and Thread

Batting and thread are important components of your quilt design. The thread you use should enhance the lines and shapes of your composition, and the batting should be an appropriate thickness.

For thread, decide if you want to match the thread to your fabric colors, or use a variegated thread to add another element of interest. I use a 40-weight thread on the top of my quilt designs because I like the definition that it gives to my stitching. Variegated thread comes in many different options, from lots of colors in the same spool to a very narrow range of values in just one color. The choice to use variegated versus one color thread is personal preference. I use both depending on what the design needs. It helps sometimes to unspool lengths of different threads

Collection of variegated threads

you are considering and lay them across your quilt top to see how the colors interact. And be willing to stop and change your mind if the thread choice doesn't seem to be working.

When I started quilting *Neon Fizz* (pages 19 and 42), I thought I would use a widely variegated thread because there were so many colors in the quilt top. But after I had stitched a line or two, I realized that it wasn't the right choice. The thread competed with the design instead of enhancing it. So I ripped it out and started again with a soft gray variegated thread that worked much better.

My favorite variegated threads are King Tut (by Superior Threads). They come in an array of beautiful color combinations and they quilt up beautifully. For single-color threads, I've begun to use Konfetti (by WonderFil Specialty Threads).

In the bobbin, I use a thinner 50-weight thread called MasterPiece (by Superior Threads). I like to use a thinner thread in the bobbin because it minimizes the risk of "eyelashes" showing on the top of my quilt. For the same reason, I always use a single-color thread in the bobbin, usually in a neutral color or one that blends with the top fabric.

I use Heirloom Premium 80/20 Cotton/Poly Blend batting (by Hobbs) or Dream Green batting (by Quilters Dream Batting), made from recycled plastic bottles. Both of these batts are low loft, so the stitching creates dimension and texture, but is easier on the machine. The small amount of polyester in the Hobbs batting helps to avoid shifting that sometimes happens with 100% cotton batts. The Dream Green batting is good for baby quilts that may get a lot of washing, and it also is less likely to crease when folded than a cotton batt.

A word about backing. I've been quilting a long time and I have a collection of fabric that reflects the different phases I've gone through on my quilting journey. I don't use printed fabrics for the fronts of my quilts very much if at all anymore, but they work great for pieced backs. Dive into your stash and find chunks of fabric that relate to the front in color or feel. Piece the chunks in a random order to create a backing big enough for your quilt. It's fun to just cut and sew without having to think too much about what goes where—it's the back after all. And you didn't have to buy more fabric.

Back of *Red Rover* with random chunks of patterned fabric sewn together to create a happy statement.

Cindy Grisdela stitching in her studio

Photo by Gregory R. Staley

Add Texture with Quilting   **87**

student GALLERY

*T*eaching is a joy for me. It's rewarding to be able to share my passion for color and Improv design with students all over the country. And teaching helps me grow as an artist too, since I have to dive deep into the structure and nuance of Improv in order to answer my students' questions and teach it effectively. Everybody wins.

I'm grateful to these students for sharing their work for this book—Denise Gossett, Elizabeth Gould, Lynne Farrow, Lynne Croswell, Monica Johnstone, Susan Koefod, and Jane Eyes.

Mondrian's Chaos by Denise Gossett, 19″ × 24″, 2020

Denise uses white effectively to define her composition.

Political Chaos by Elizabeth Gould,
quilted by Krista Moser, 57″ × 57″, 2018

**Elizabeth created repetition in her curved
shapes and variety in the different sizes.**

Piazza by Elizabeth Gould,
quilted by Krista Moser, 41″ × 49″, 2018

**An Improv block design is activated with a
stitching motif of lines and pebbles.**

Log Cabin Improv by Lynne Farrow,
40″ × 40″, 2019

**One Improv block is set off with
asymmetrical stripes in Lynne's design.**

Garden Improv by Lynne Farrow,
15″ × 22″, 2019

Lynne uses Improv stripes and
curved lines to create her landscape,
enhanced with interesting stitching
by hand and machine.

Pharm Improv by Lynne Farrow, 21˝ × 28˝, 2020

A low saturation color palette with white makes the lines and shapes stand out.

Cabin Fever
by Lynne Croswell,
27˝ × 42˝, 2020

Black-and-white checkerboard stripes add an unexpected element of surprise to Lynne's composition of Improv puzzle blocks.

Acid Gothic by Monica Johnstone, 24″ × 39″, 2020

An acid green background and curved arch shapes add interest to Monica's Improv block and curve design.

Improvisation Jazz by Susan Koefod, 19″ × 26″, 2019

Susan used print fabrics with Improv Curves, Angled Stripes, and Curved Strips. Red adds the spark.

Walk in the Woods by Susan Koefod, 11″ × 47″, 2019

A nicely unified design with repetition of angled stripes in the center and Improv curves on the outside.

Crossroads by Jane Eyes, 27″ × 27″, 2020

Jane chose a symmetrical balance and added half-square triangles to make her Improv puzzle design her own.

RESOURCES

Here are a few of my favorite books on quilting and design.

Art Quilts International, by Martha Sielman (Schiffer Publishing)

Color: A Workshop for Artists and Designers, by David Hornung (Laurence King Publishing)

Create Your Own Free-Form Quilts, by Rayna Gillman (C&T Publishing)

Cut-Loose Quilts, by Jan Mullen (C&T Publishing)

First Steps to Free-Motion Quilting, by Christina Cameli (Stash Books)

Free Expressions, by Robbi Joy Eklow (Quilting Arts LLC)

Free-Motion Quilting with Angela Walters, by Angela Walters (Stash Books)

Gee's Bend: The Architecture of the Quilt, by Paul Arnett, et al. (Tinwood Books)

Liberated Quiltmaking, by Gwen Marston (American Quilter's Society)

The Magical Effects of Color, by Joen Wolfrom (C&T Publishing)

Nancy Crow, by Nancy Crow (Breckling Press)

Quilters Playtime, by Dianne S. Hire (American Quilter's Society)

Scrap Quilts: The Art of Making Do, by Roberta Horton (C&T Publishing)

Thinking Outside the Block, by Sandi Cummings with Karen Flamme (C&T Publishing)

A Treasury of Amish Quilts, by Rachel and Kenneth Pellman (Good Books)

ABOUT THE AUTHOR

Cindy Grisdela has been making things since she was a child. Her mother taught her to sew as soon as she was old enough for her foot to reach the pedal of the sewing machine, and some of her fondest memories are of time spent in the fabric store immersed in color and pattern.

Cindy made many traditional quilts early on in her quilting journey while she worked as a financial journalist and later raised two boys. Being an artist at heart, eventually she grew tired of following patterns and longed to create quilts that were uniquely hers. Not knowing exactly where to start, she began by first tweaking old favorite patterns, such as Log Cabin and Drunkard's Path, before finally evolving into a more contemporary, improvisational style that speaks to a modern aesthetic.

Photo by Phil Grisdela

Jessie, studio supervisor and quality control expert

Photo by Cindy Grisdela

Working improvisationally, she cuts lines and shapes directly out of fabric freehand, without a pattern or template. The design process unfolds organically, as each decision about color and line influences the next. She doesn't know exactly what the finished composition will look like, and that's fine with her. The process of discovery is what makes Cindy excited to step into her studio every day. "What if …?" is her favorite question.

Color and texture are the focus of Cindy's work. The color is the starting point for almost all her designs. Although she is known for her bright colors, she enjoys challenging herself to use new color palettes that might be outside her comfort zone. The texture is the second step. Cindy does all her own free-motion stitching freehand on her BERNINA, without a computer or marking ahead of time.

Cindy is a full-time artist and teacher. She travels all over the country lecturing and giving workshops on Improv design to quilt guilds and groups. Helping students let go of the rules to uncover and explore their own creativity is a great joy for her. She has appeared on *Quilting Arts TV* and contributed to *Quilting Arts* magazine, and she is a Juried Artist Member of Studio Art Quilt Associates. Cindy is also an instructor on the innovative and interactive platform Creative Spark Online Learning (by C&T Publishing).

Also by Cindy Grisdela:

Visit Cindy online and follow on social media!

WEBSITE
cindygrisdela.com

INSTAGRAM
@cindygrisdelaquilts

CREATIVE SPARK
creativespark.ctpub.com